GEORGETOWN

Meditation on a Bicentennial

Photography by Robert Llewellyn
Text by Timothy Healy, S.J.

Copyright © 1989 by Georgetown University Press. Photographs Copyright © 1989 by Robert Llewellyn. All rights reserved. This book, or any portion thereof, may not be reproduced in any form without permission of the publisher, Georgetown University Press. Photographs may not be reproduced in any form without the permission of Robert Llewellyn.

Published by Georgetown University Press, Georgetown University, Washington, DC 20057. Library of Congress Catalog Card Number 89-2089. ISBN 0-87840-484-8. Printed in Japan by Dai Nippon Printing Co., Ltd. First edition.

Designed by Timothy J. Ward.
Edited by Michael D. Feinstein.

GEORGETOWN

Meditation on a Bicentennial

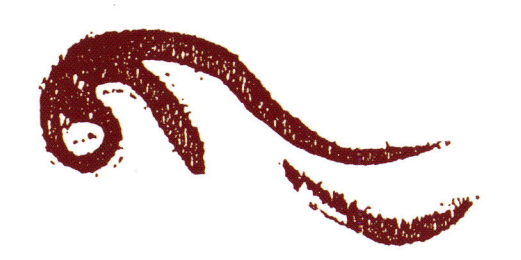

ROBERT LLEWELLYN *Photography*

TIMOTHY HEALY, S.J. *Text*

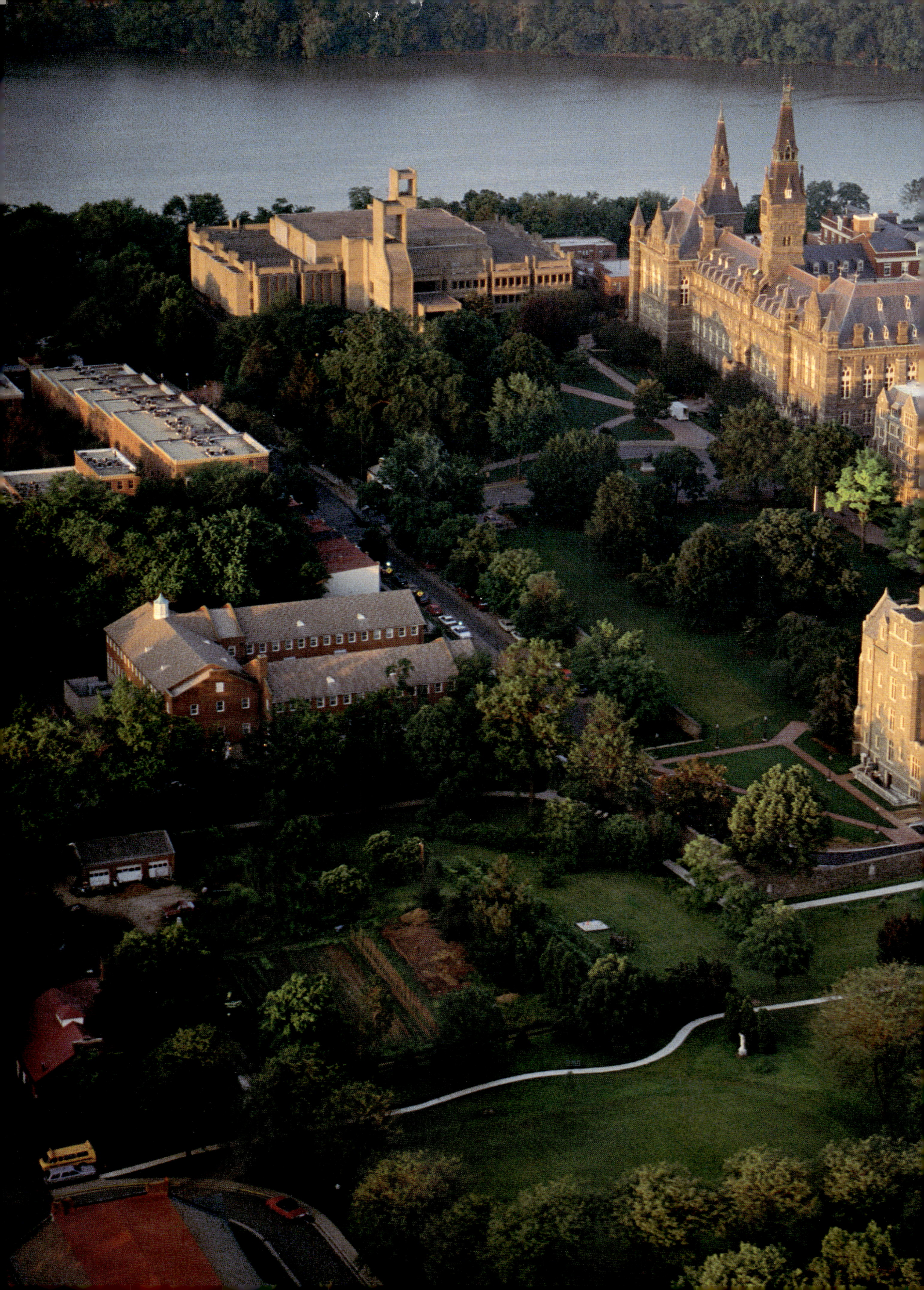

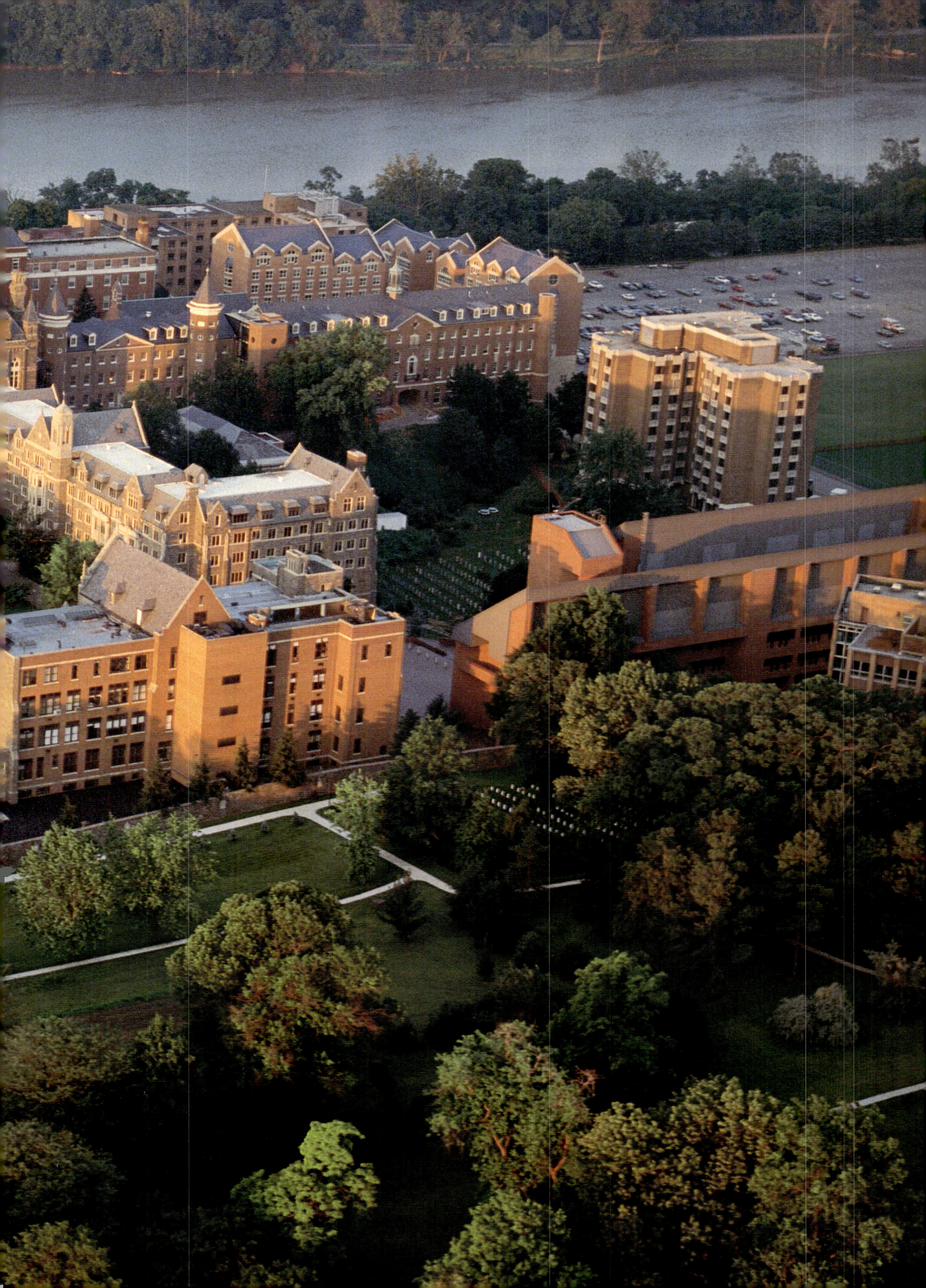

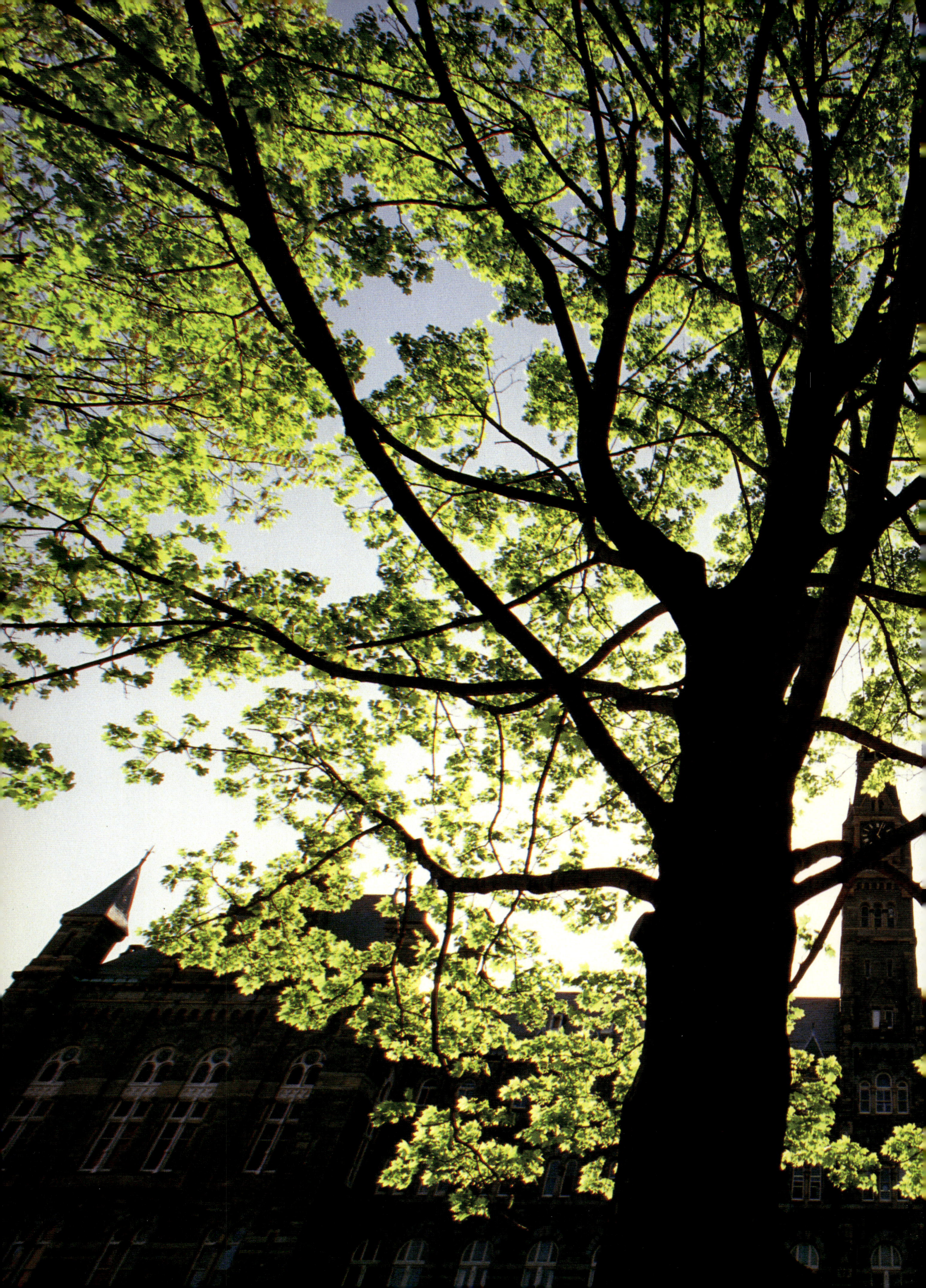

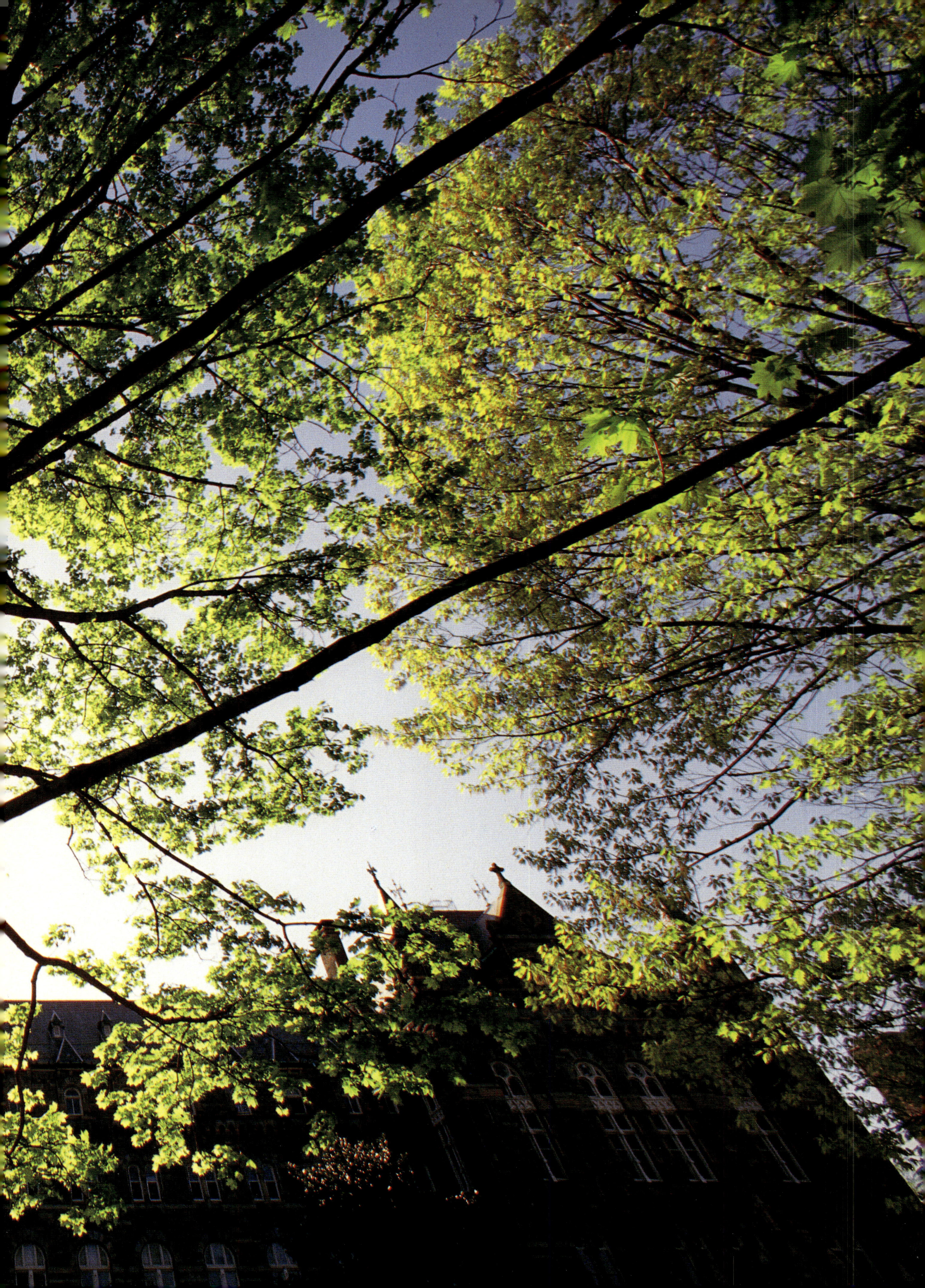

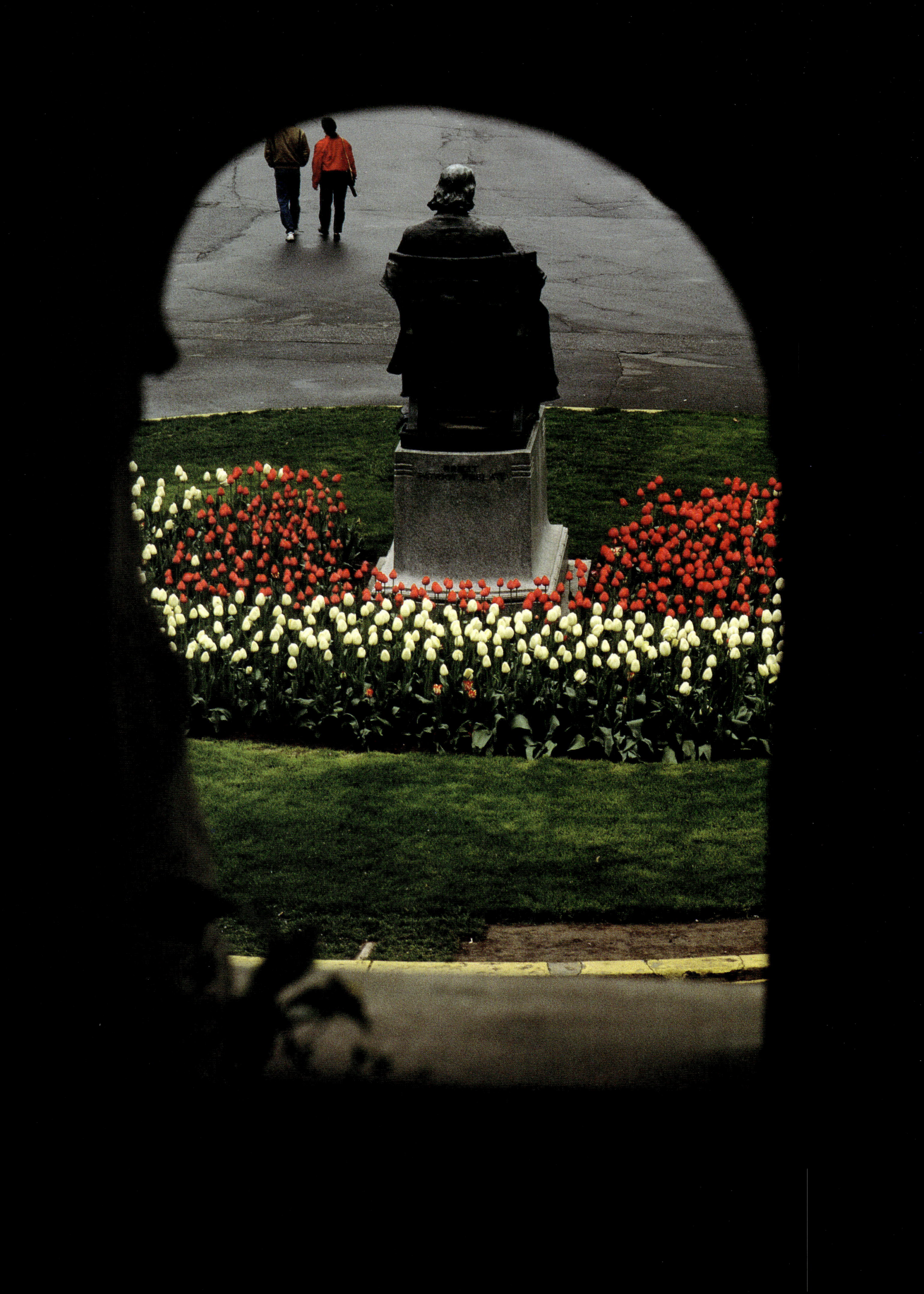

IN THE SPRING OF 1788 John Carroll wrote, "We shall begin the building of our Academy this summer . . . on one of the most lovely situations that imagination can frame." It is hard to think back onto that spacious century's open ground – but the lovely situation that Carroll found had three elements: a hill, a river and a city.

The hill that Carroll chose for his academy is no mountain, and thus does not fall under Chesterton's stricture that in God's plan mountains are to be looked up to not down from. It is rather a minor bump along the banks of the Potomac, nowhere near as high as the neighbor hill on which the National Cathedral sits. Perhaps Carroll was willing to sacrifice height for nearness to the river. He also must have known in his bones that it is proper for cathedrals to dominate skylines, but not for universities.

On the East Coast, hills argue to stability, very much in the scriptural sense, since they don't bounce around much. Ours recalls for us the long continuity of university work. The

[generations]

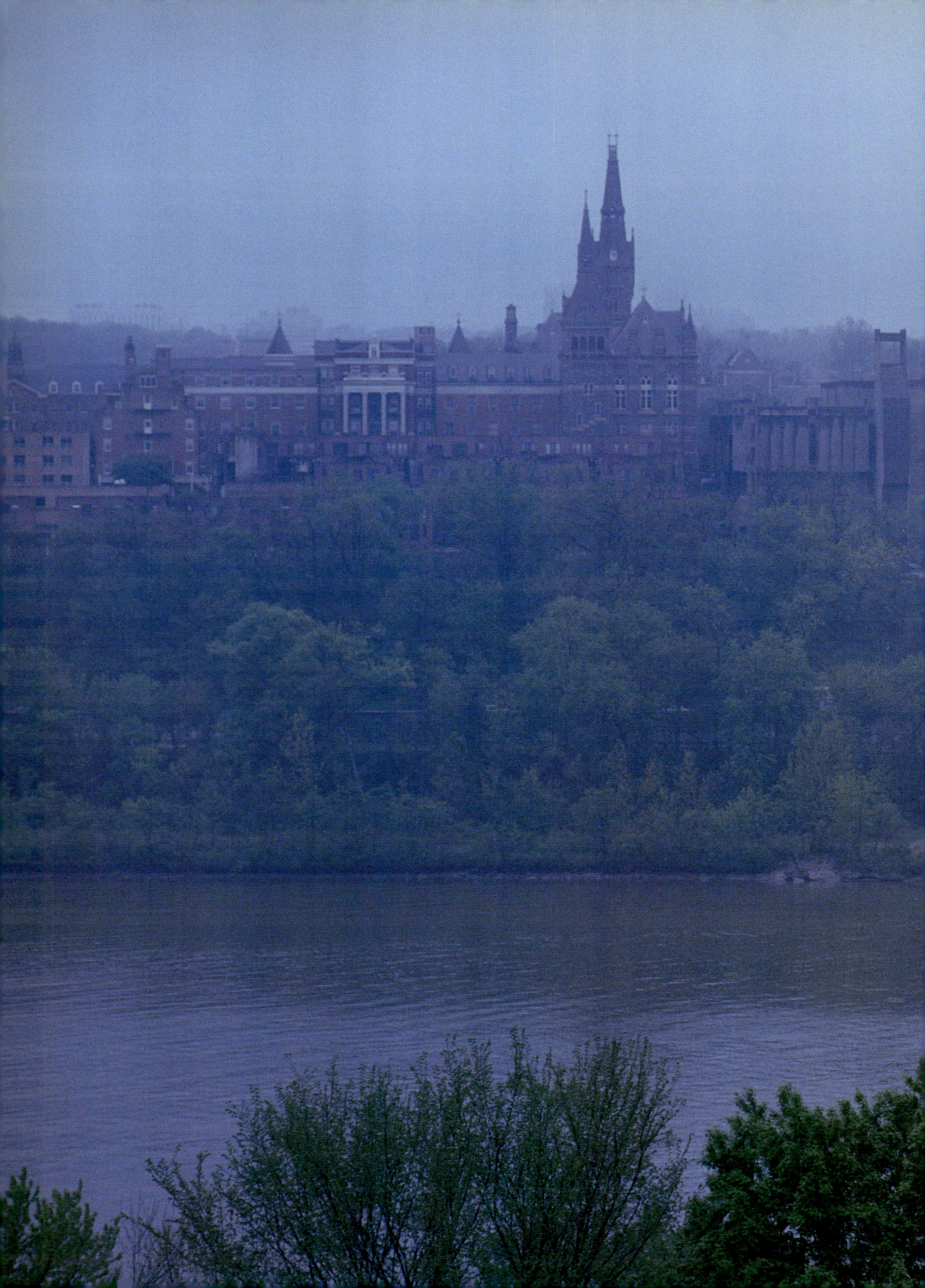

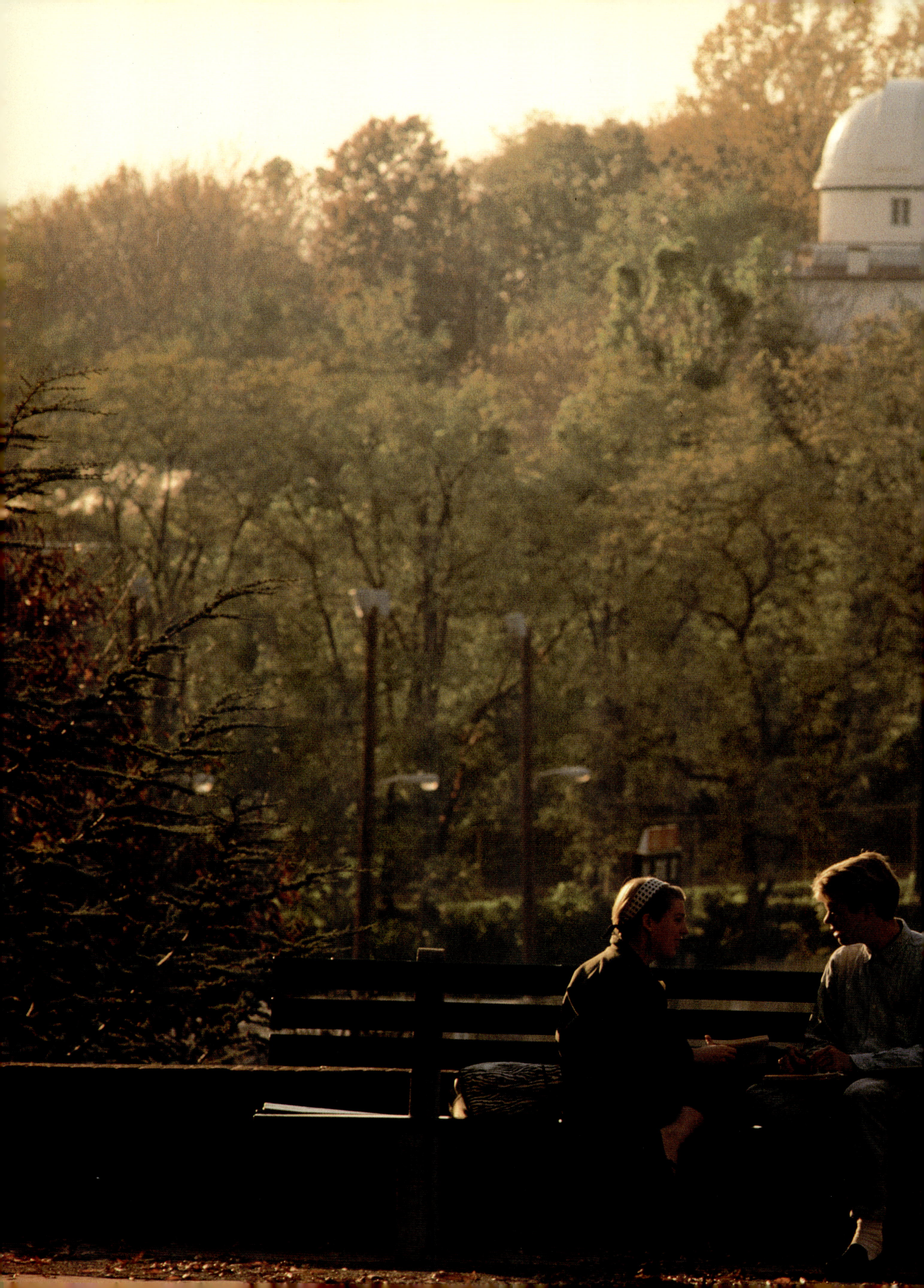

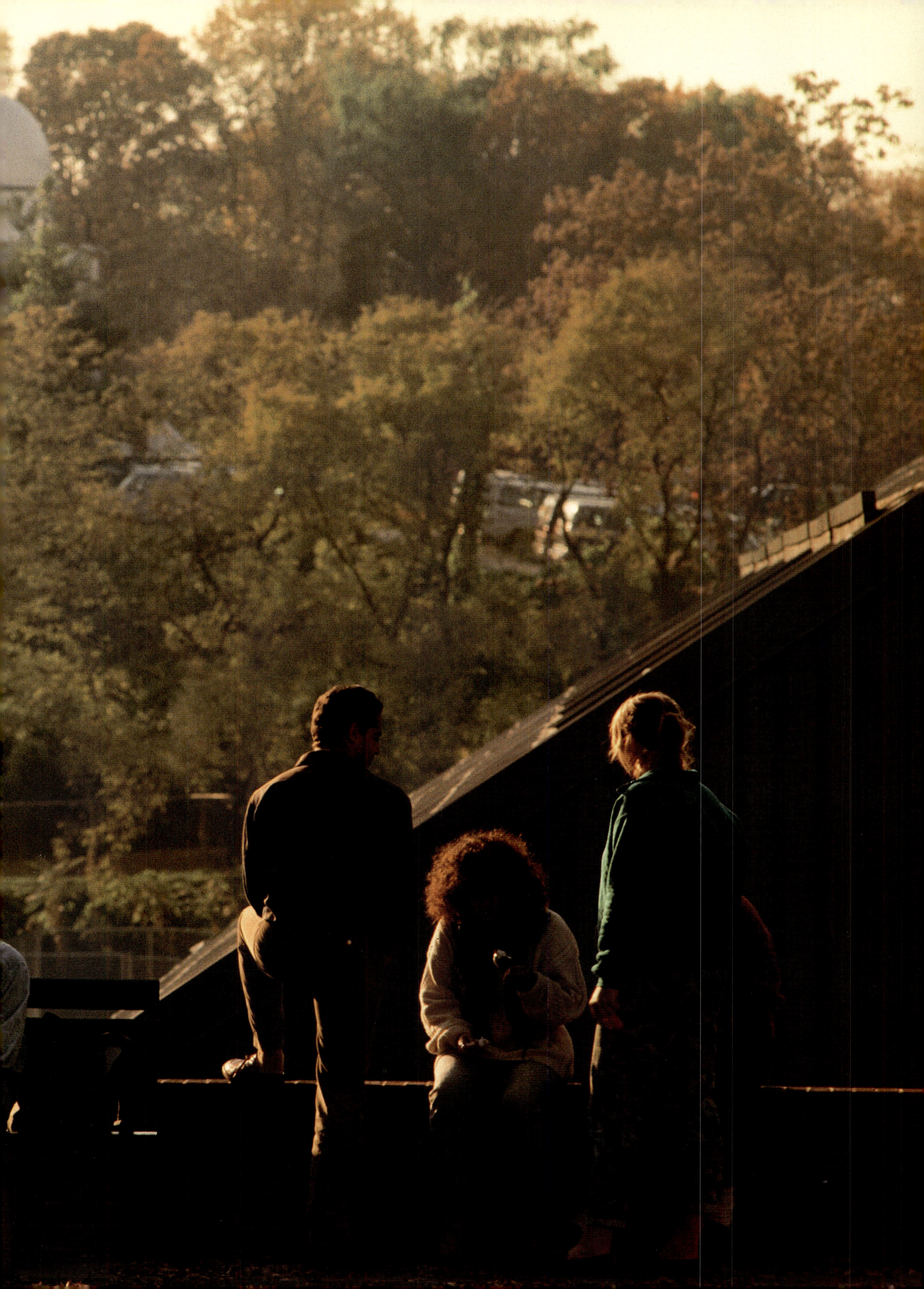

generations of the young change in style, but the problems and promise of growing into citizenship don't, and the faculty, a self-perpetuating body, is in one sense both timeless and ageless.

Faculty, with their teaching and research, make the great stability on this ground. Georgetown gathers a galaxy of different studies, and thus works on the ancient claim of our Latin title, "universitas studiorum" – to encompass the whole world of ideas. That encompassing is of course a dream, and no university has ever made it real, but in our fractured world the dream matters.

Our hilltop also recalls two centuries of Catholic faith and worship on this steady platform that reaches modestly towards God. John Carroll would have been quite at home with us today, in Dahlgren Chapel, in the easy talk among students and faculty, in the prayer and lives of his brother Jesuits, in the long flow of God's grace across this good ground.

Like many ancient universities, Georgetown is "river rounded." The 1796 seal of the University describes us as "apud ripas Potomaci," on the banks of the Potomac. Universities are places of change and the classical image of life and its vagaries is a river. Rivers have their own rhythms,

[sometimes]

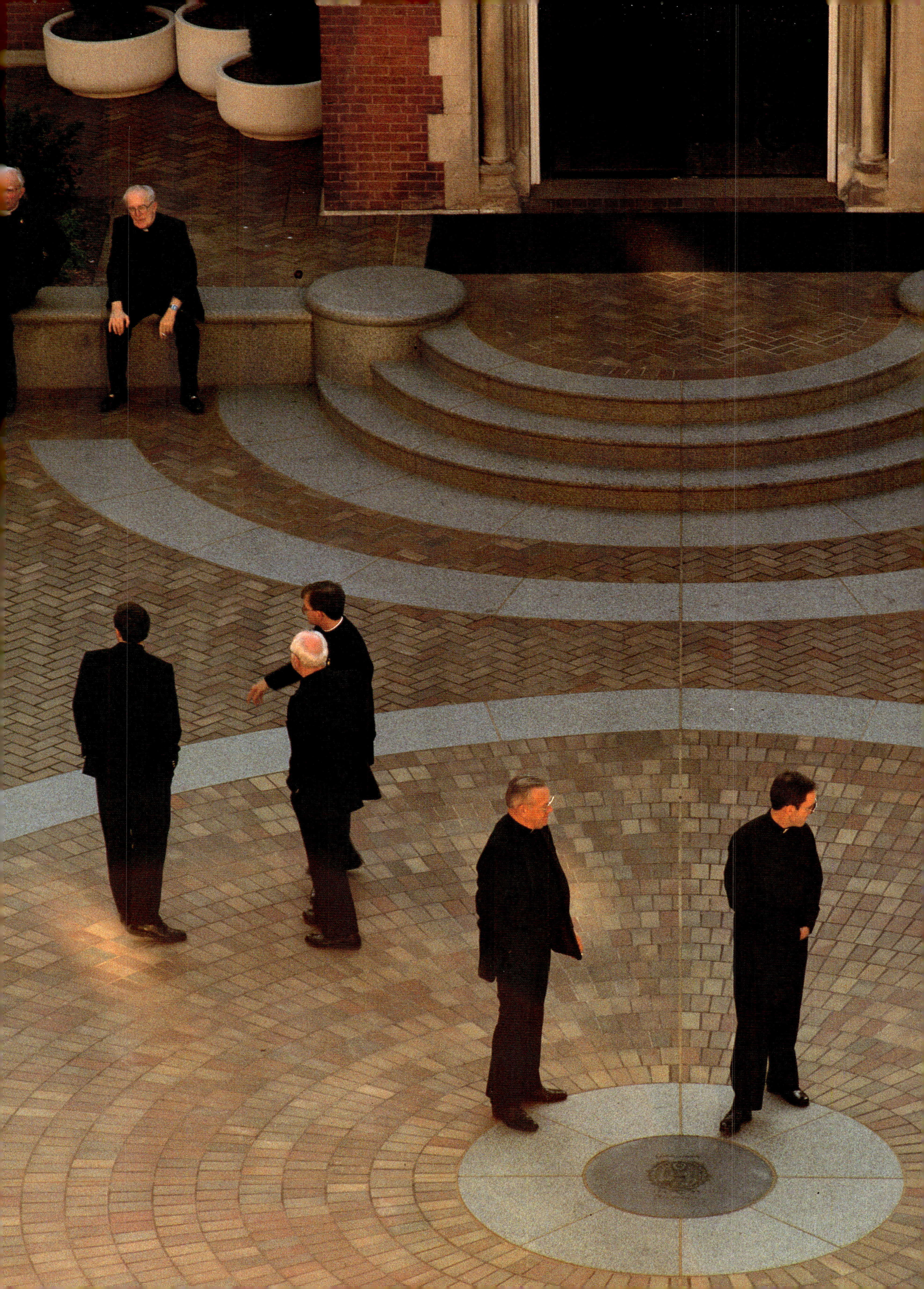

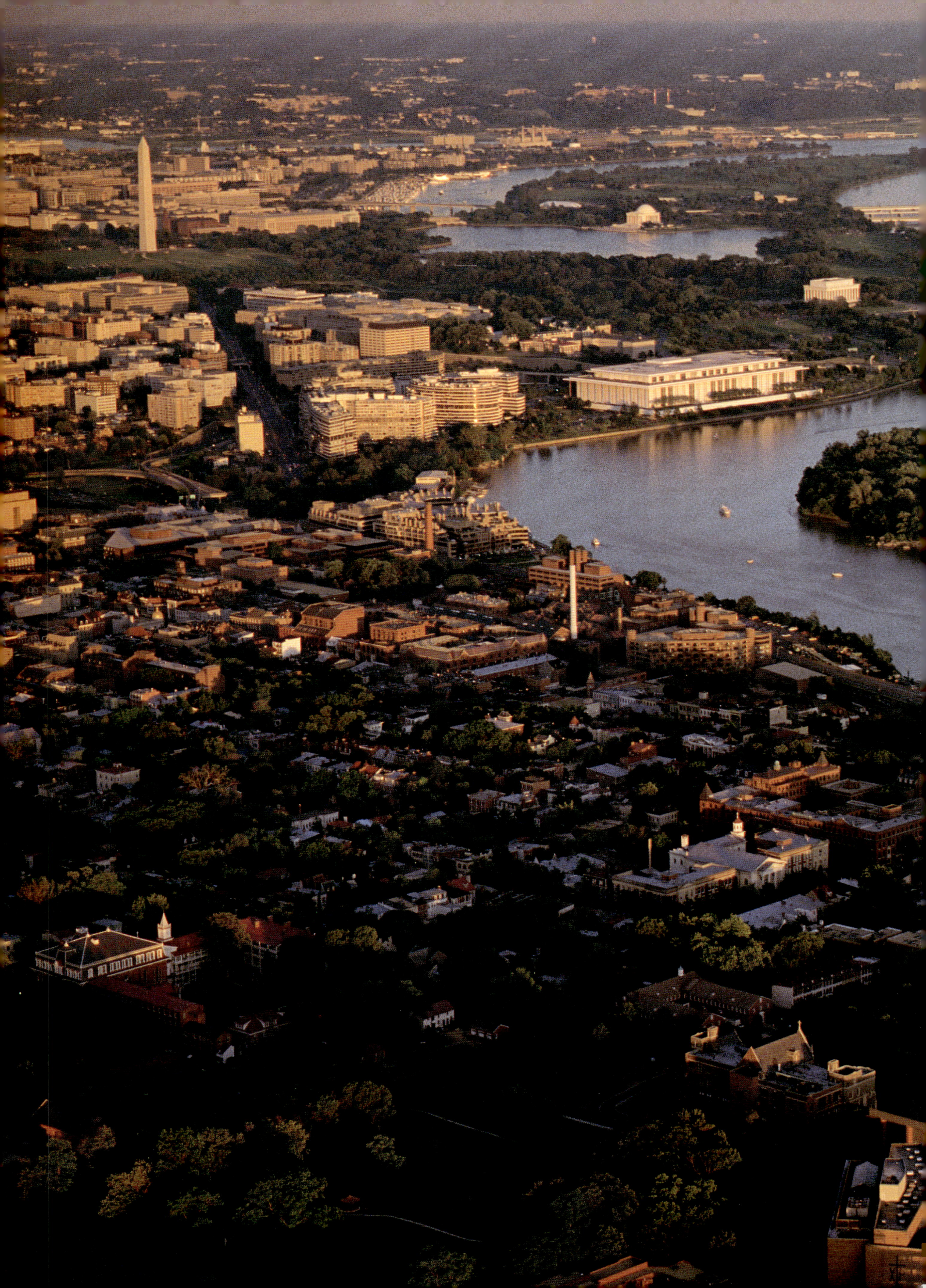

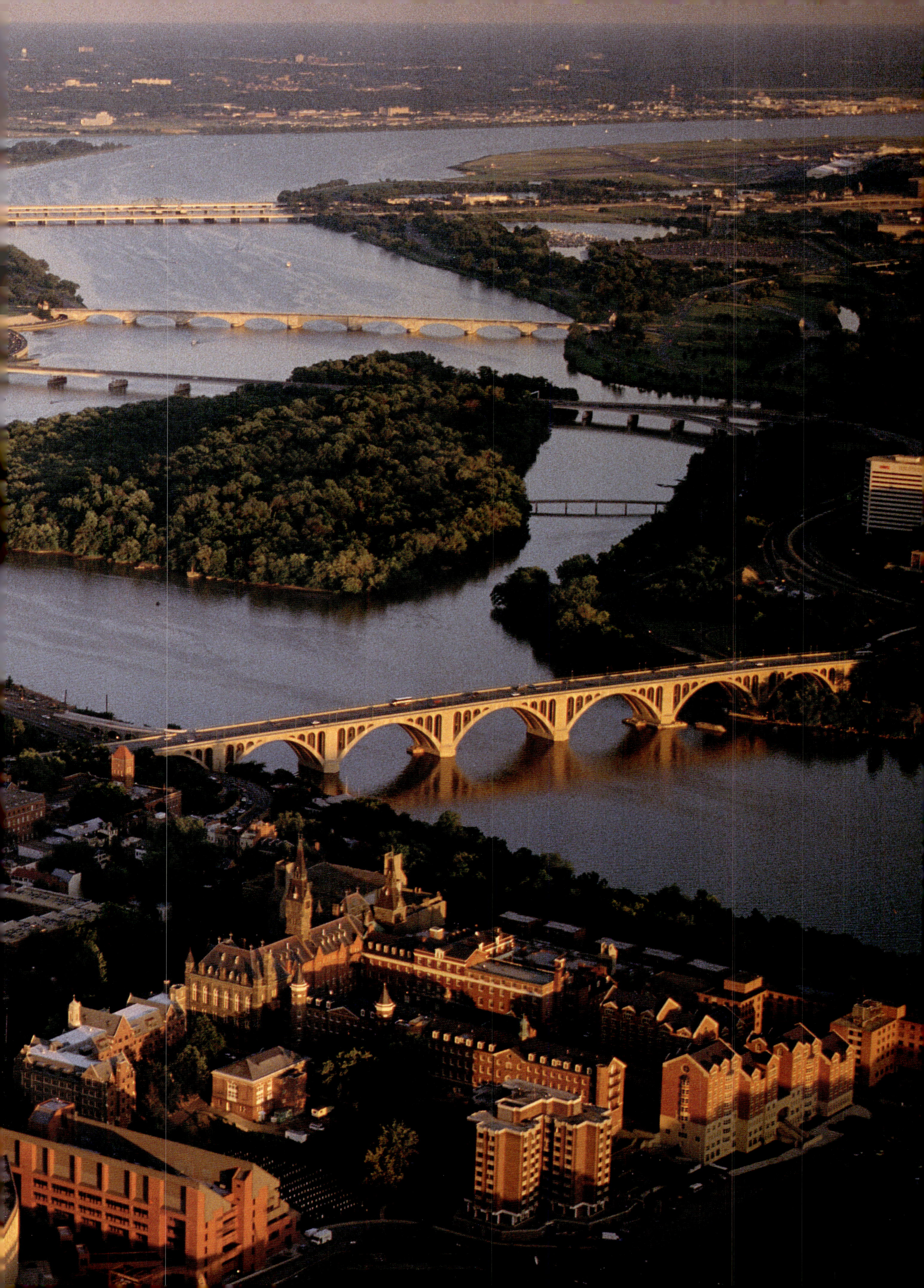

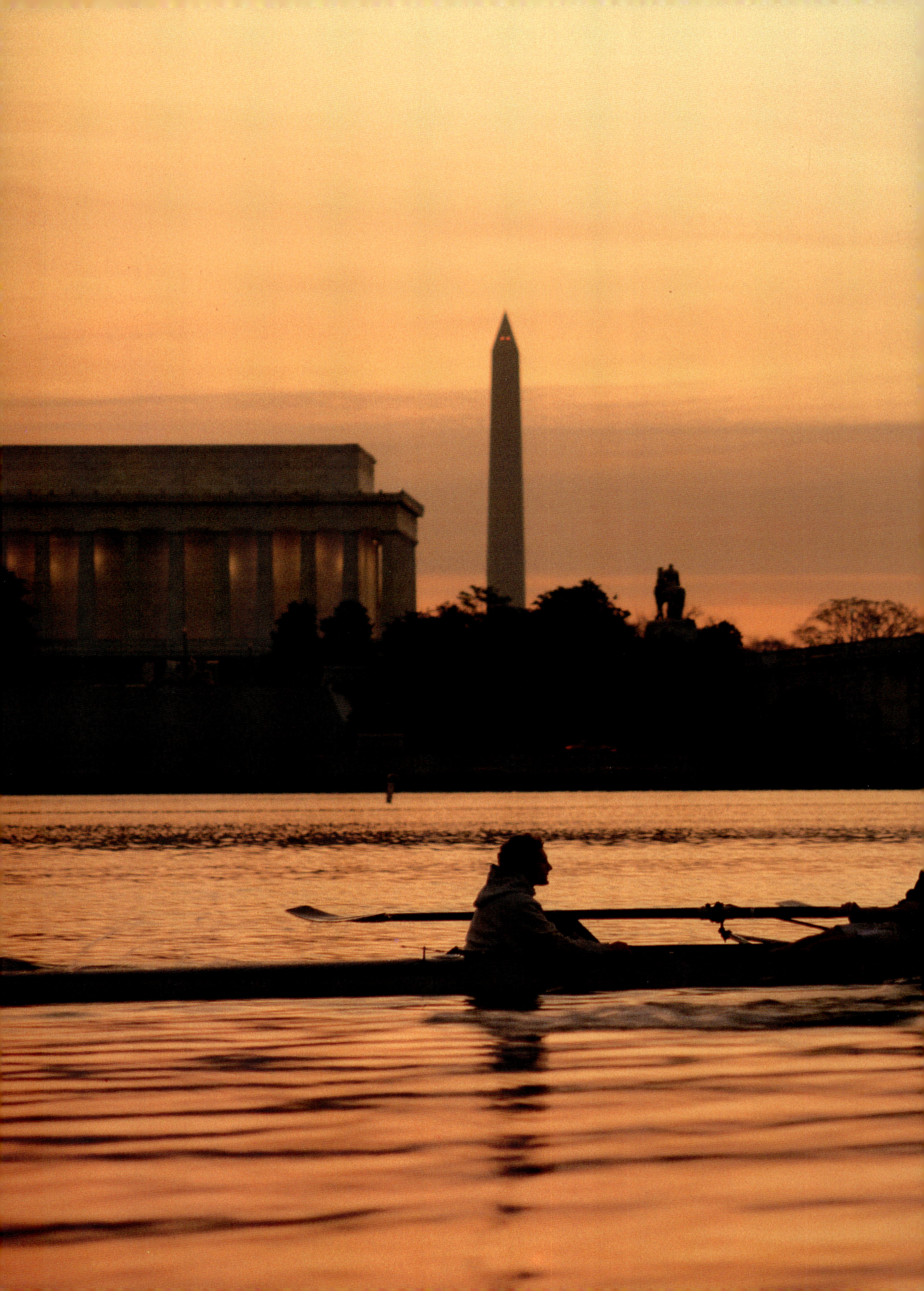

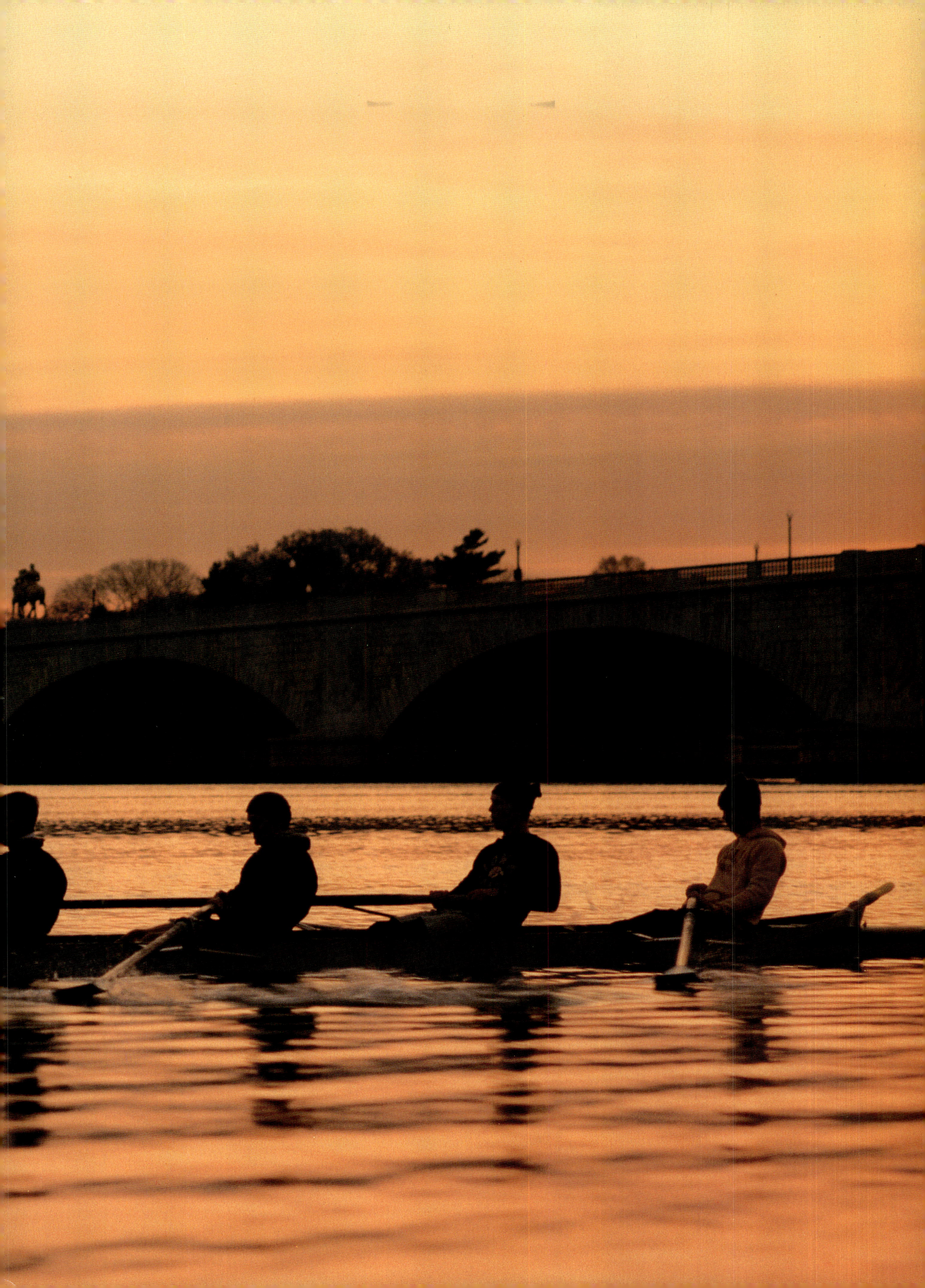

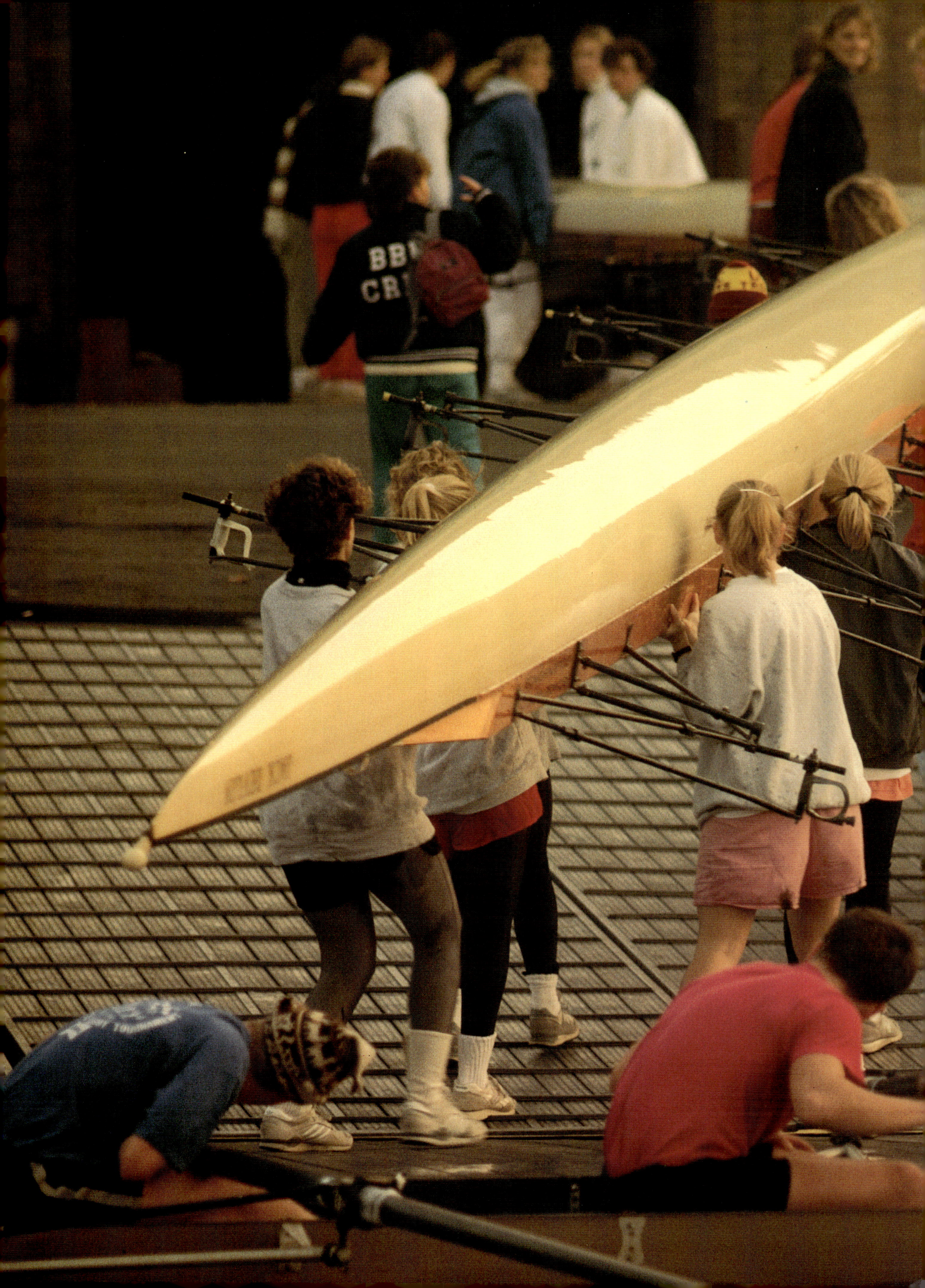

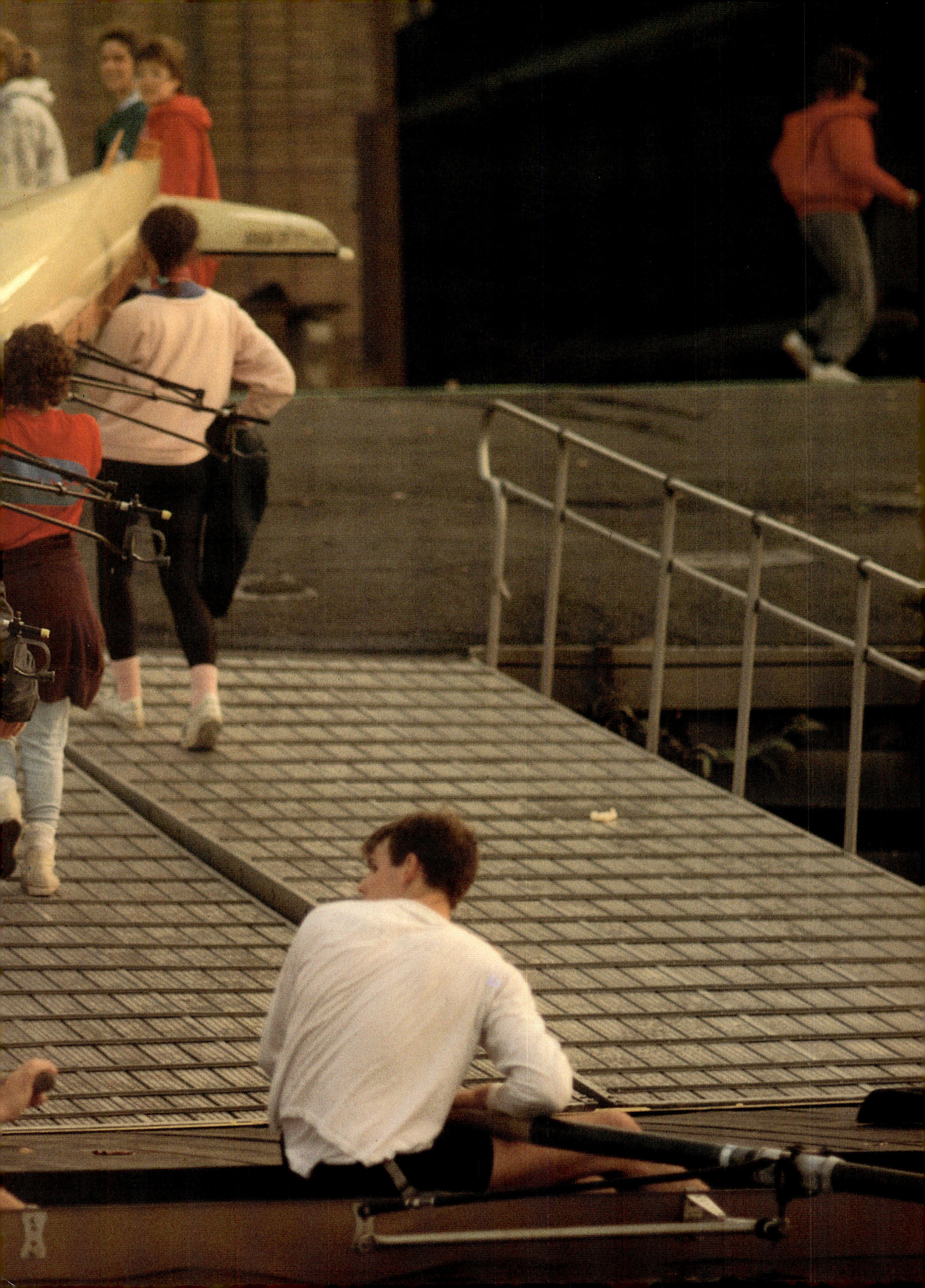

sometimes sluggish and smooth, sometimes swift and dangerous. Like all great rivers the Potomac served us first as a boundary, then for long years "useful, untrustworthy" it carried our trade into the Bay and out to sea. For a century now, in the morning and afternoon, it has been pocked by the beat of our rowers' eights and fours. It is always present to us, brooding, quiet, a thing of beauty and a barrier.

The river is a good image for our changing young, shining, restless, "watching and waiting" as they poise towards the larger waters that await them. Styles come and go. Hair, like skirts, lengthens and shortens, musical forms have a life-cycle of a lustrum, and students can talk airily of generations passing between freshman and senior year. But like a river, their very flow makes for a kind of liquid continuity that can bear on its surface the little wisdom and much learning of a university. River and hill go well together. They balance rock and water, stand and flow.

Carroll could hardly have anticipated the District of Columbia, now crowding its arbitrary boundaries and fingering its suburbs deep into Maryland and Virginia. He knew the seaport of George Town with its quiet ways but he could never have imagined the monstrous cuckoo that landed in its nest,

[the Federal]

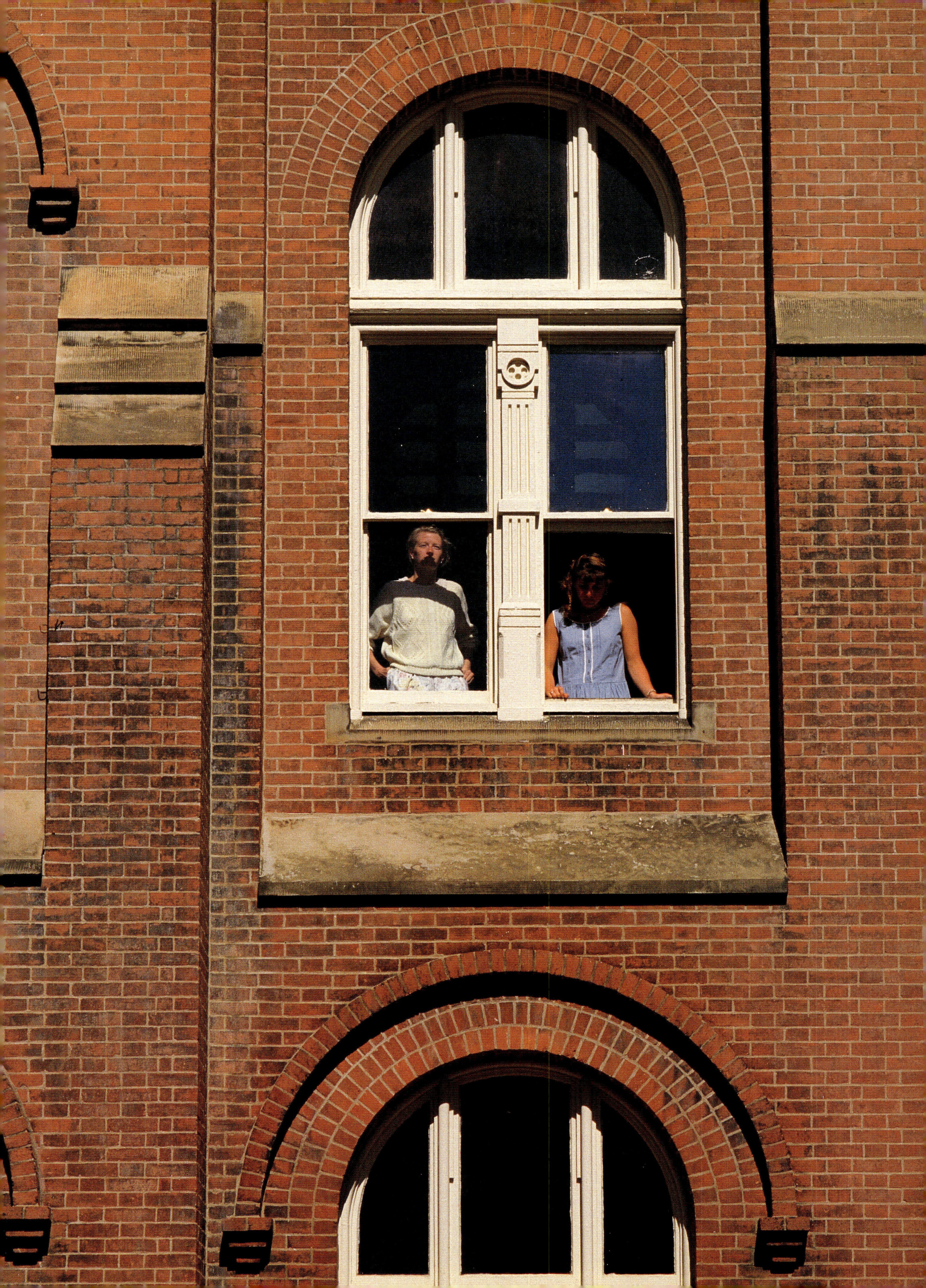

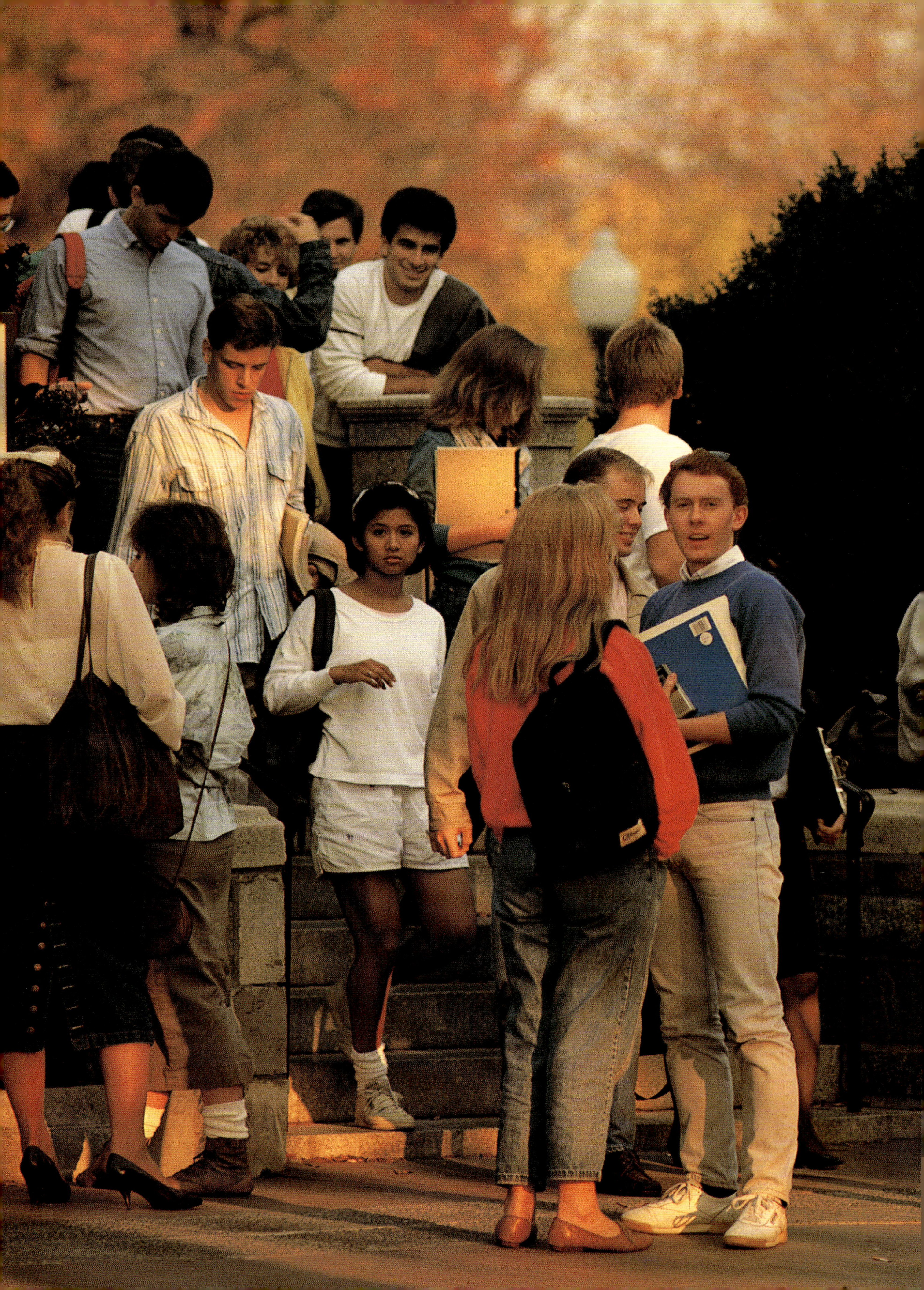

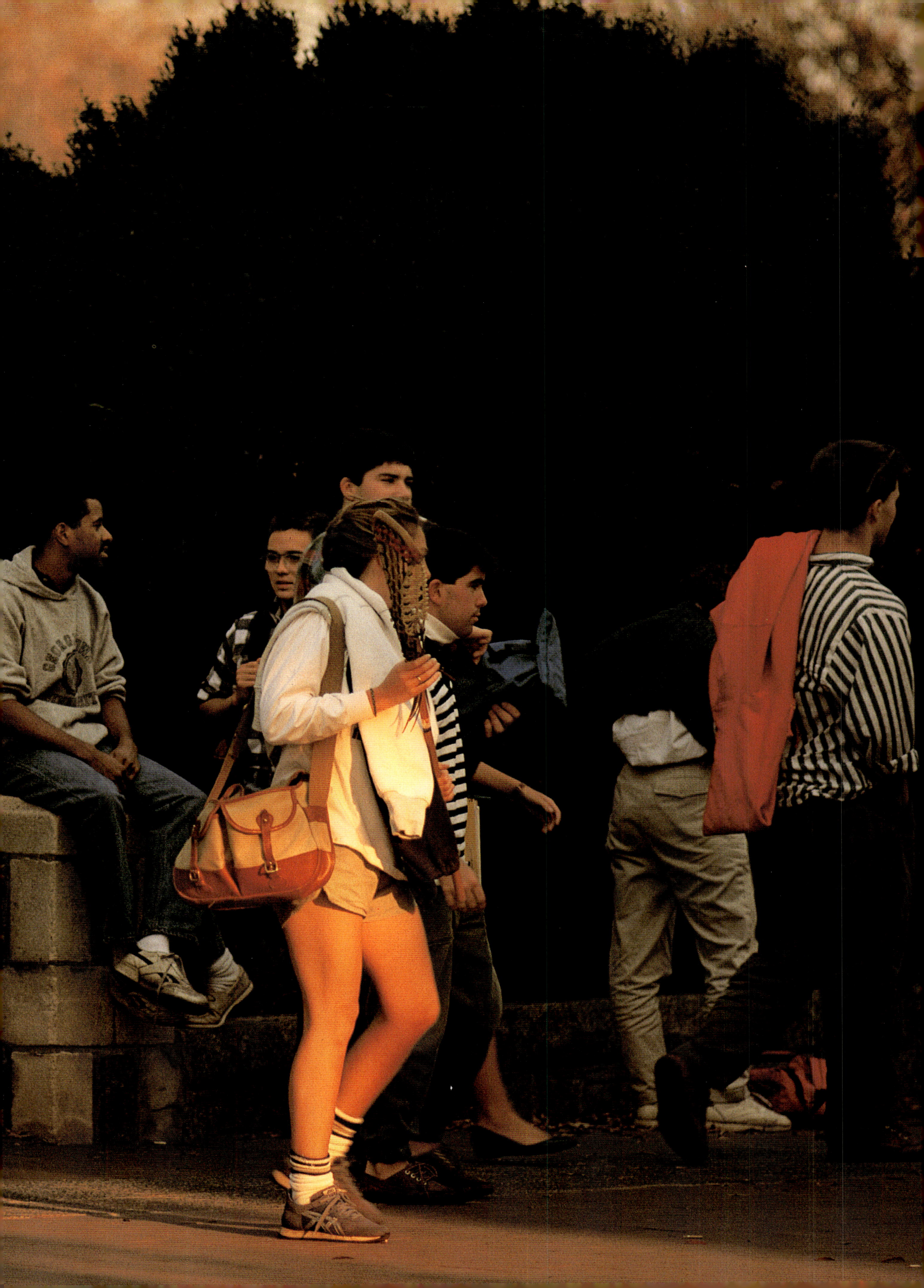

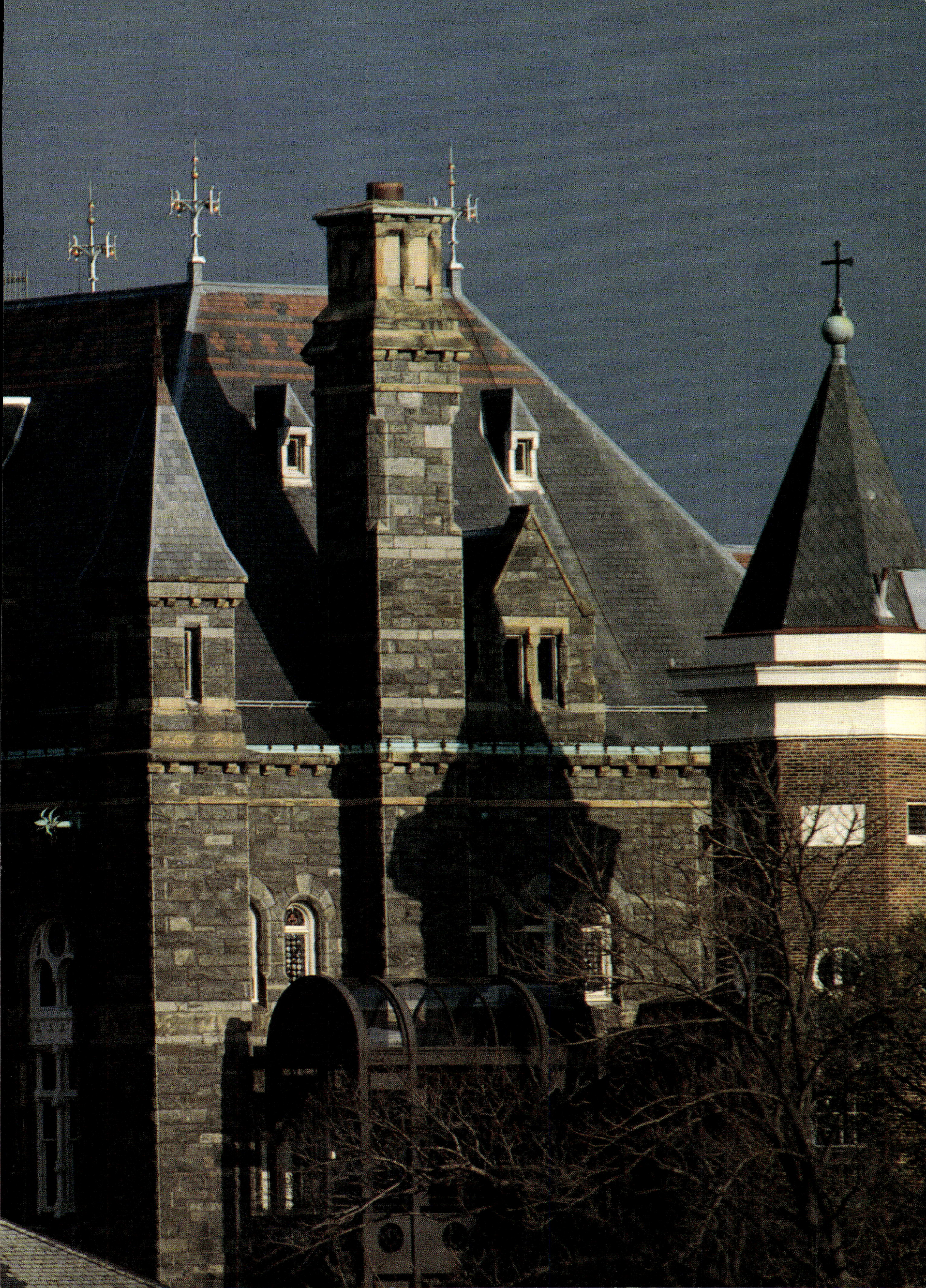

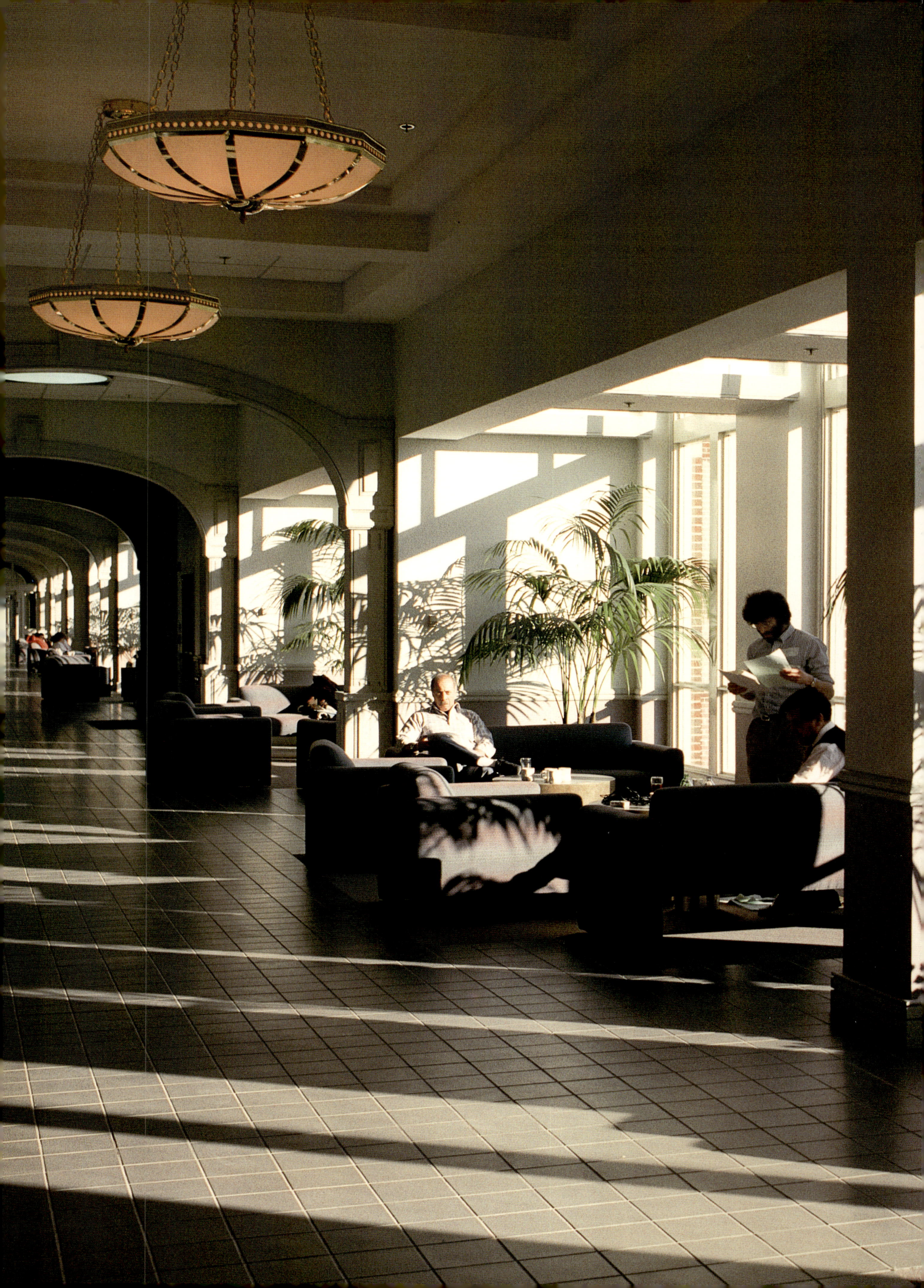

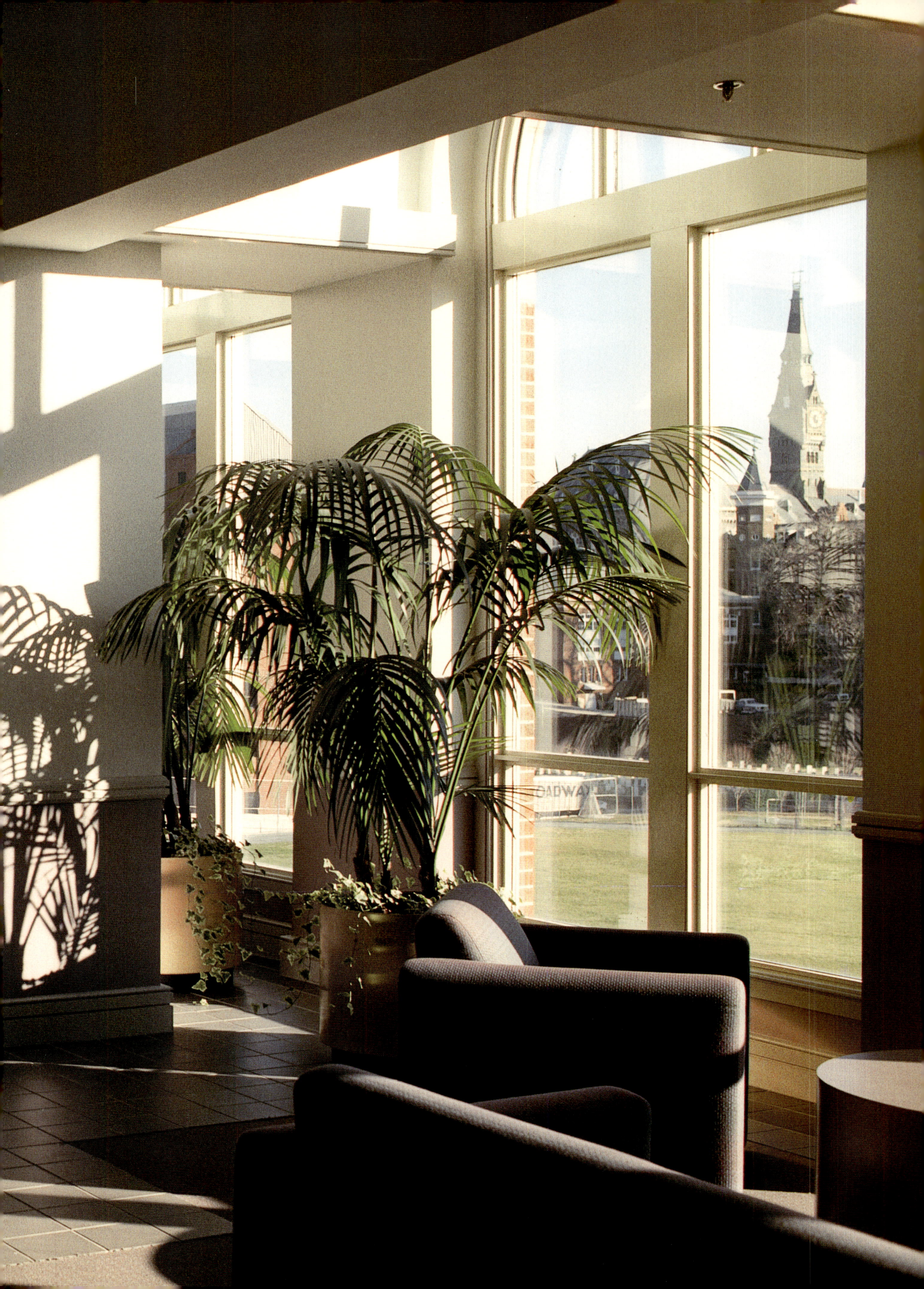

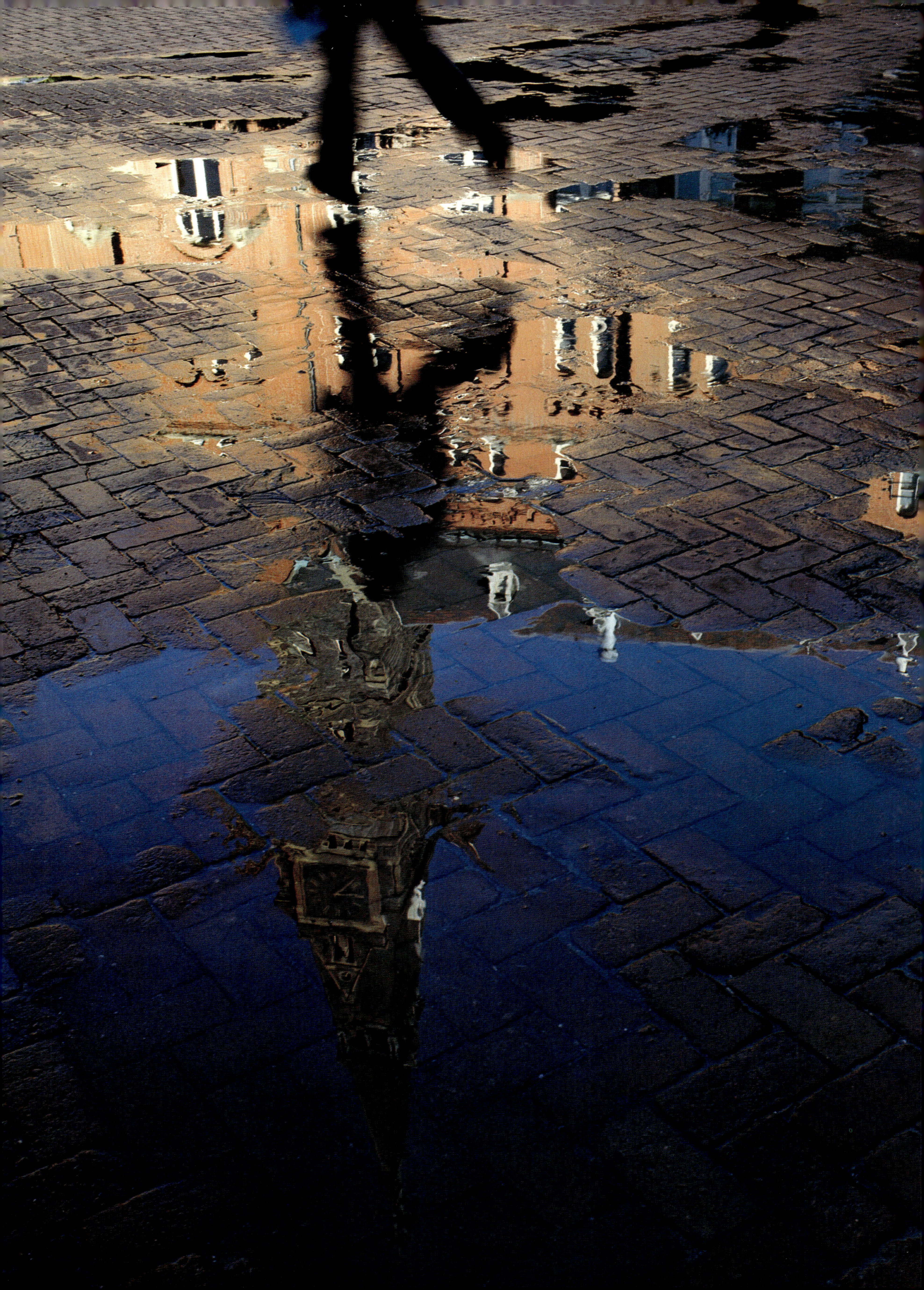

the federal government. The Civil War set Washington fast as the eye of federal power, and since then the District's reach has extended to cover a continent and indeed the world. Carroll did foresee its grasp of a nation, but he never dreamt of how its words and deeds would circle the globe.

It used to be fashionable for universities to guard their "coped and poised towers" from the "base and brickish skirts" that surround them, but Georgetown has chosen not to do this. The reason for that choice is quite simple. Over two centuries our city has grown in size, but it has also grown in need. The District of Columbia has one of the highest per capita incomes in the world, and also one of the largest number of citizens on welfare in the nation. There can be no paltering with our obligations to serve the place and the people where and among whom God set us.

The federal cuckoo in our nest has probably given more shape to Georgetown than any other force brought to bear on it. Young Americans are fascinated by government and its workings, and Georgetown's young yield to that fascination by the hundreds every year. In vain the University warns that "Potomac fever," when caught early, is incurable. For the hundreds of students who work on "The Hill" or in the

[bureaucracy]

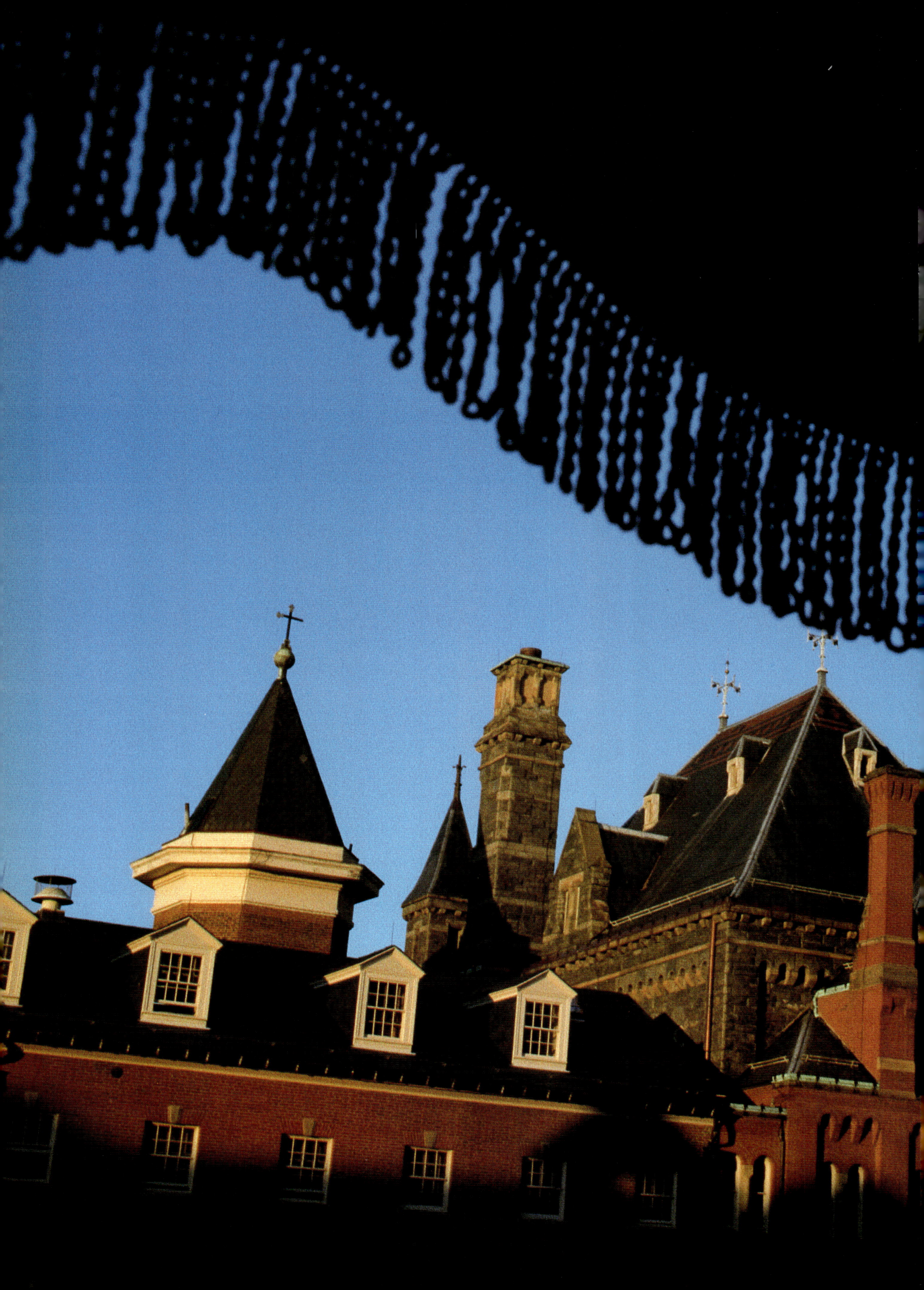

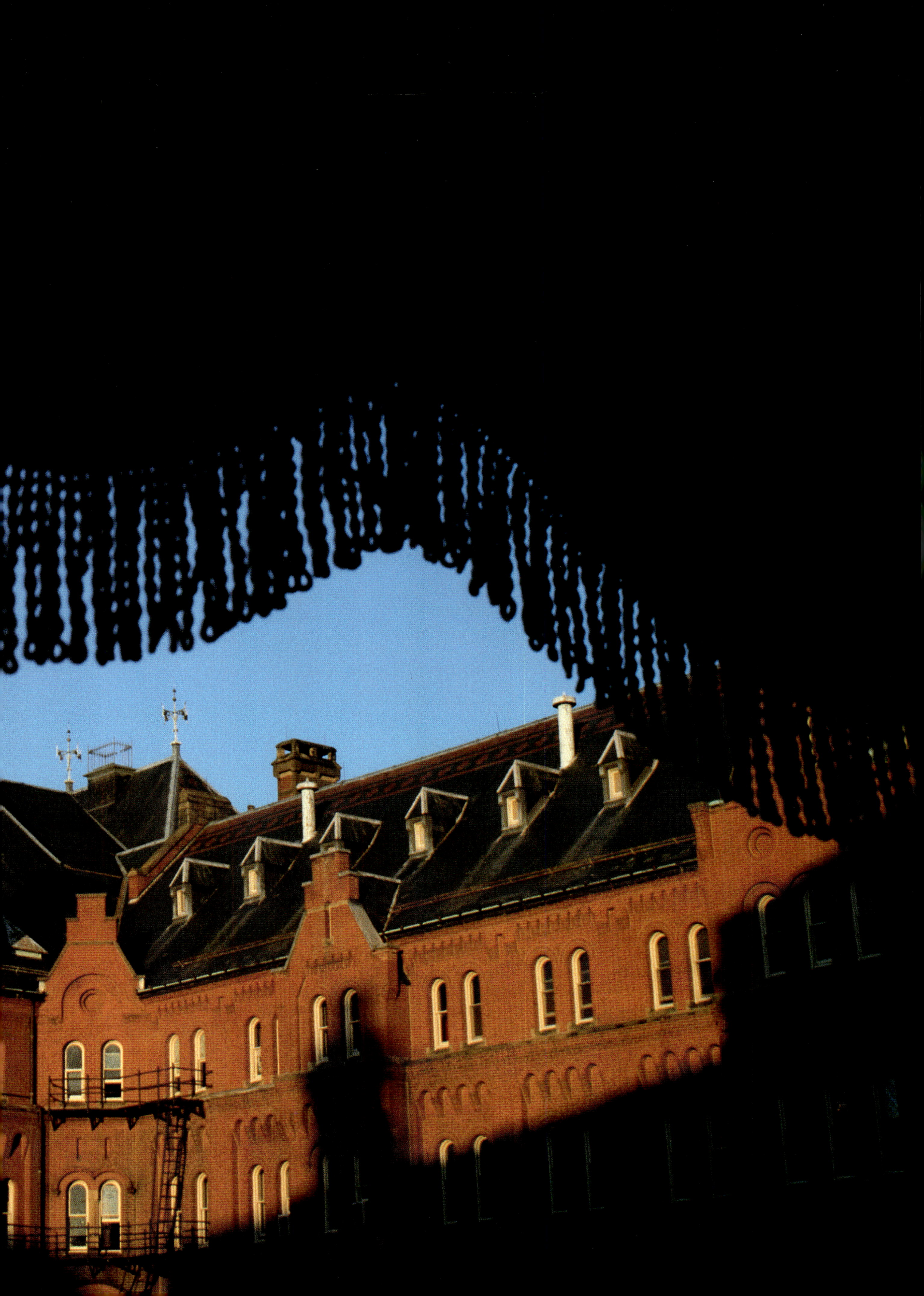

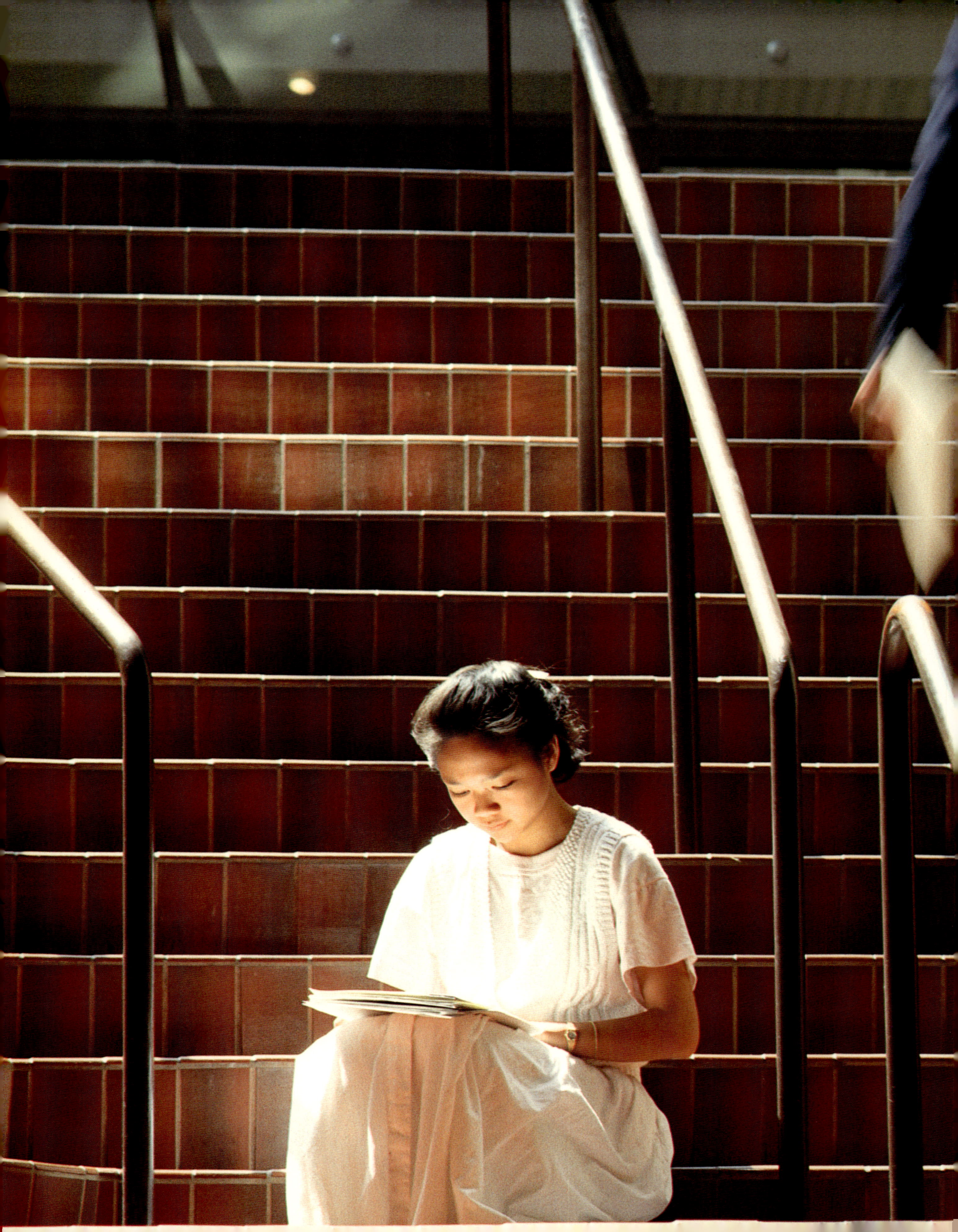

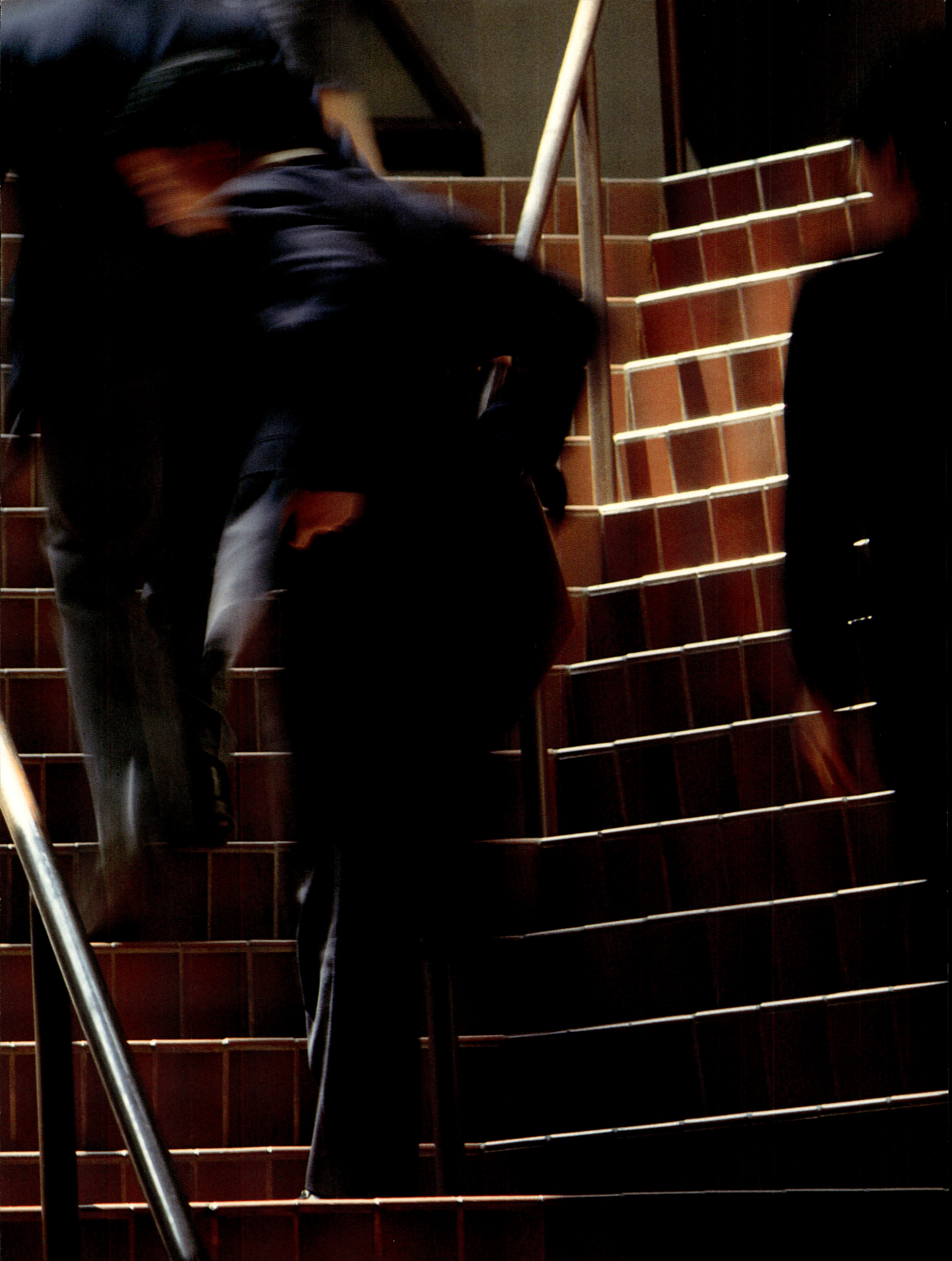

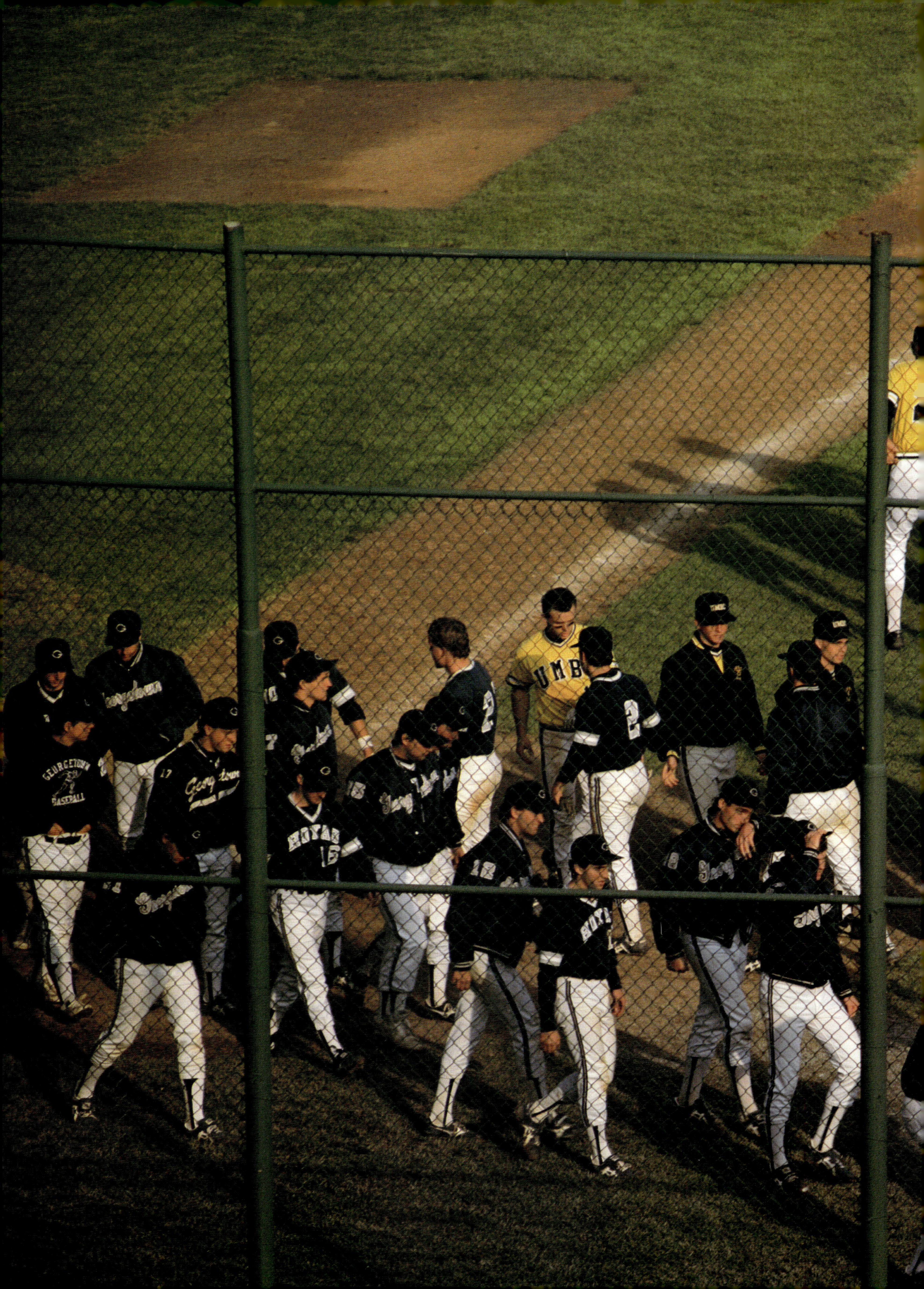
GEORGETOWN
BASEBALL
HOYAS
UMBC

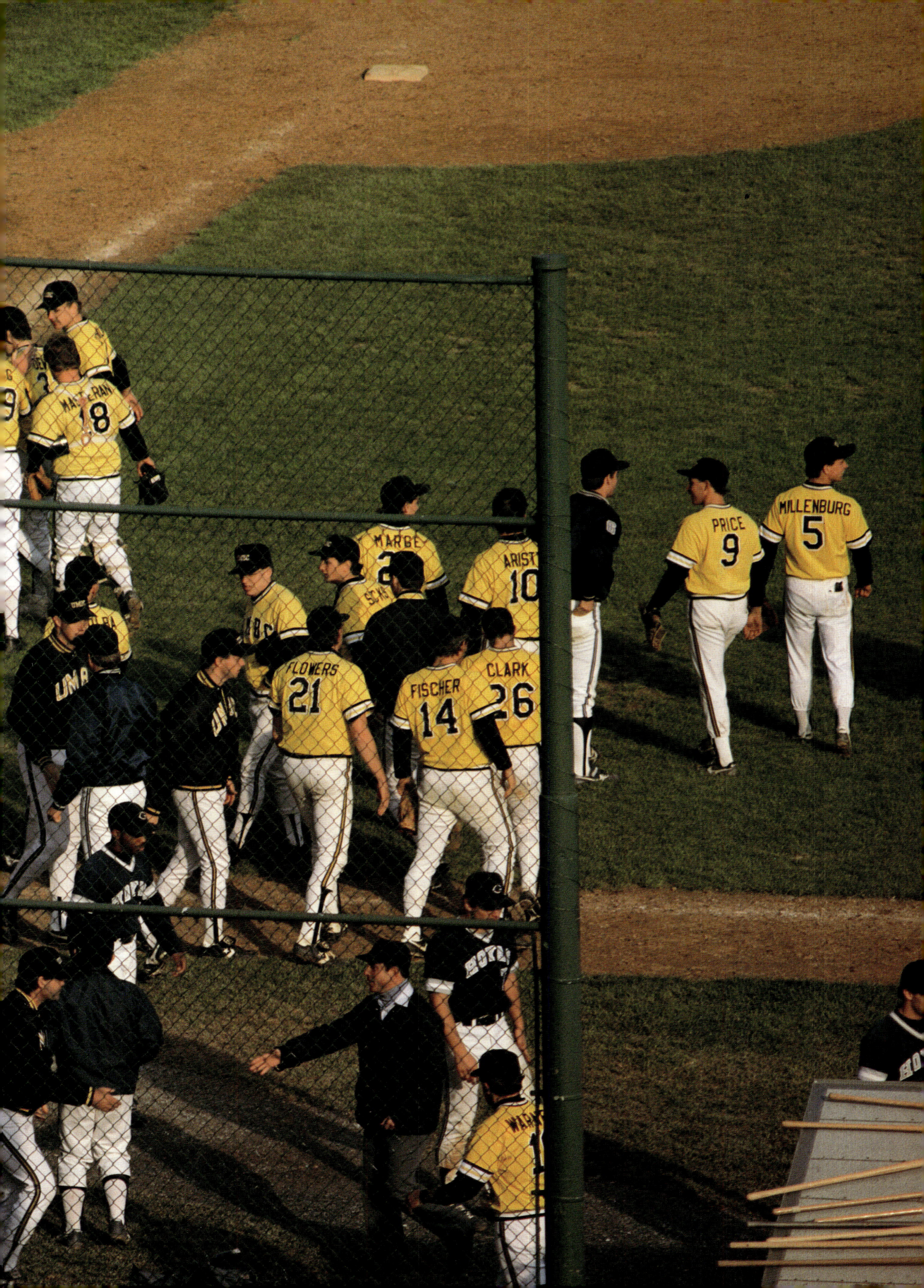
MILLENBURG
5
PRICE
9
FLOWERS
21
FISCHER
14
CLARK
26

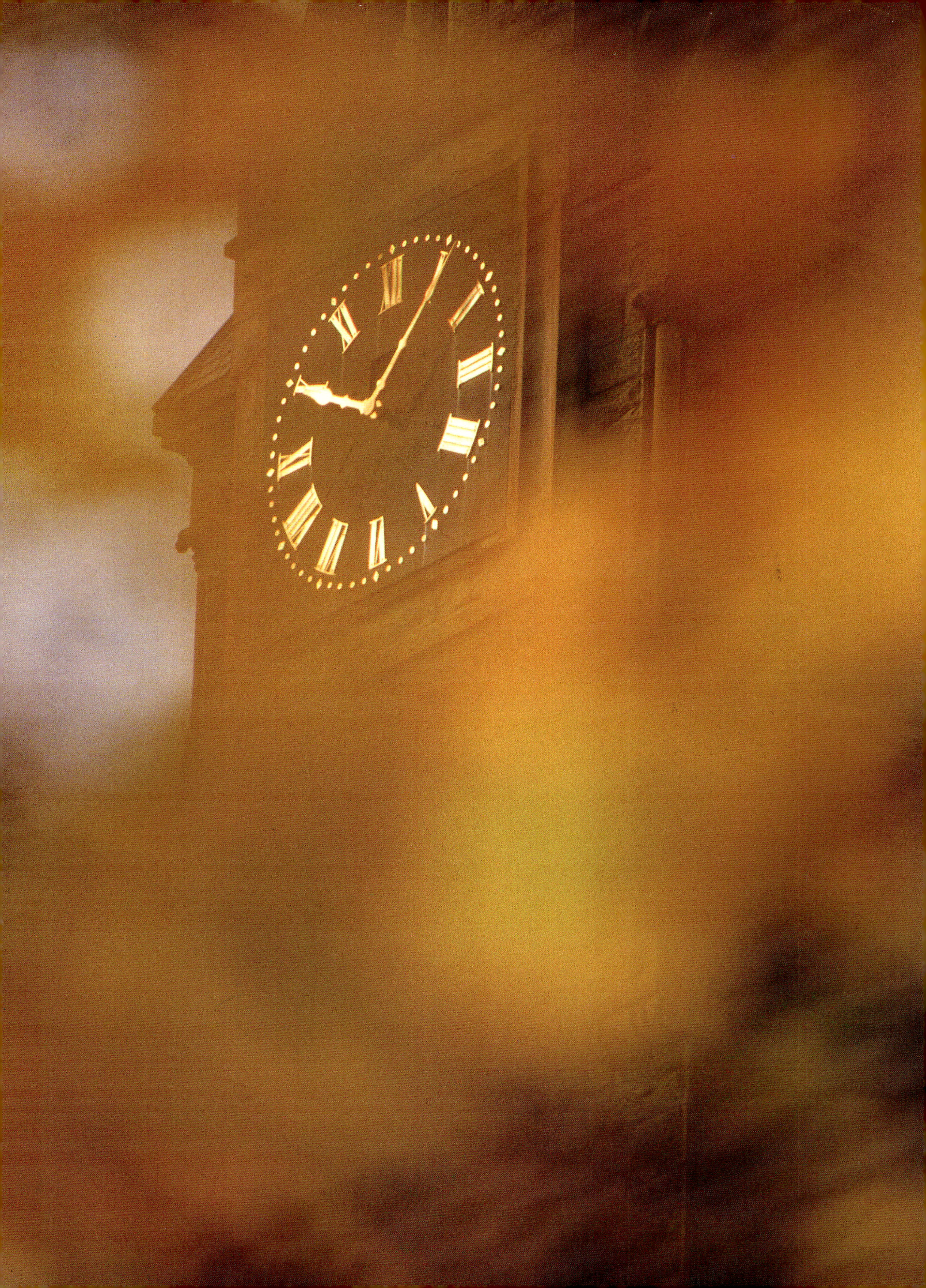

bureaucracy, anywhere indeed in the federal Escorial, Georgetown does not need to lift a finger to rivet them for life to the innards and habits, as well as, thank God, to the dreams of democracy.

To hill and river and city – we must add the dimension of time. We began six years after the Treaty of Paris, and thus Georgetown still keeps a touch of Carroll's Revolution. We look for future citizens and leaders, trained in this lively capital of American life, trained not as servants to its political assumptions but as workers of change, as critics and analysts, as shapers of a new America for a new century. Carroll also dreamt of bringing to bear upon the universal Church the strength of republican process and of sharing with it what he called "the good effects of freedom." Georgetown's men and women must bring that same dream, strength and freedom to the work of building a Church for the 21st century.

In both tasks Georgetown wrestles with the question, "How do you tell the dancer from the dance?" Any university is a work of time and its first task is learning. In order to learn we gather ourselves, from the nation and the world. Out of that gathering comes an immediate good for our city. Students tutor, renew housing, man soup kitchens and visit the old. In a

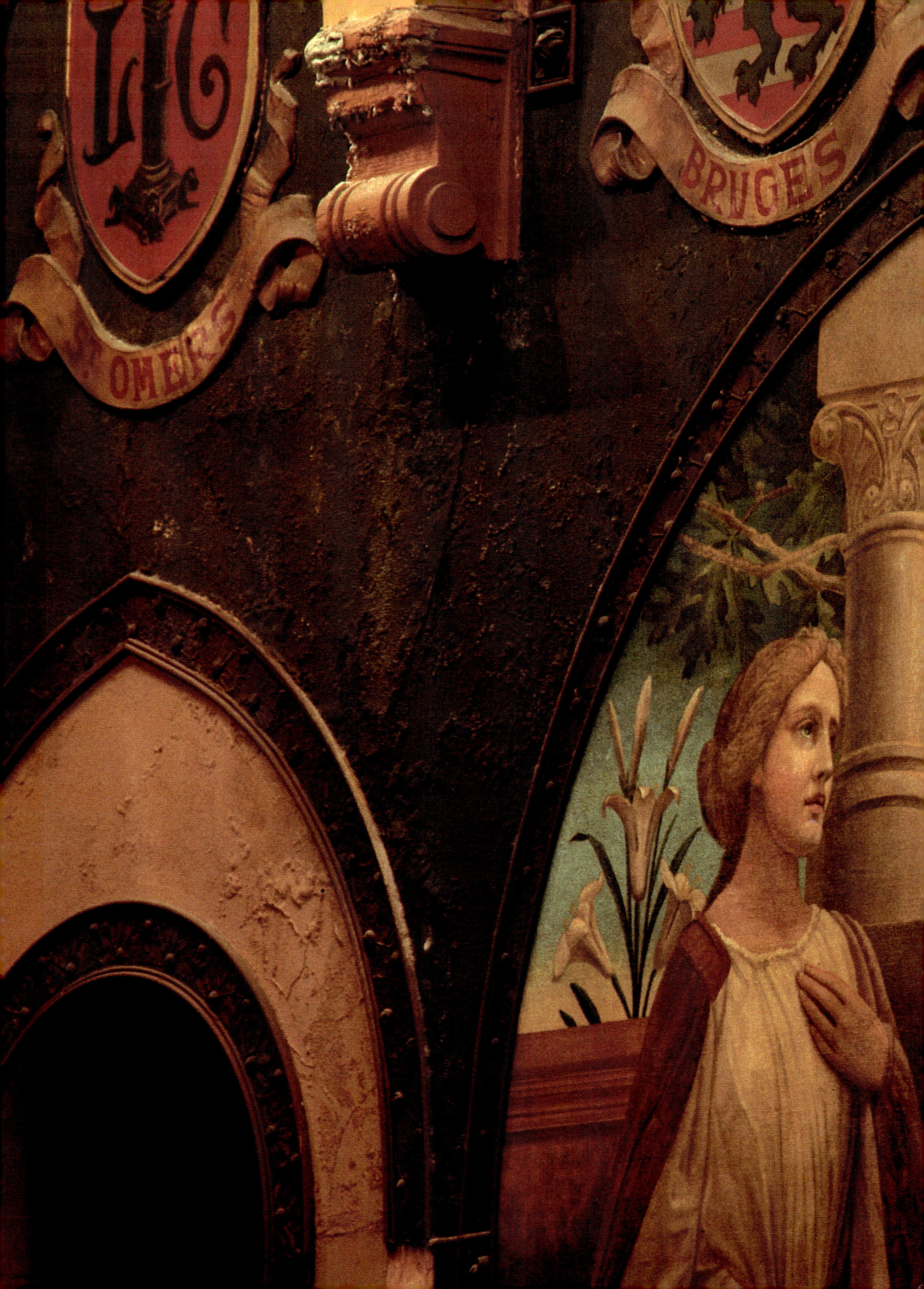
ST OMERS
BRUGES

LIEGE

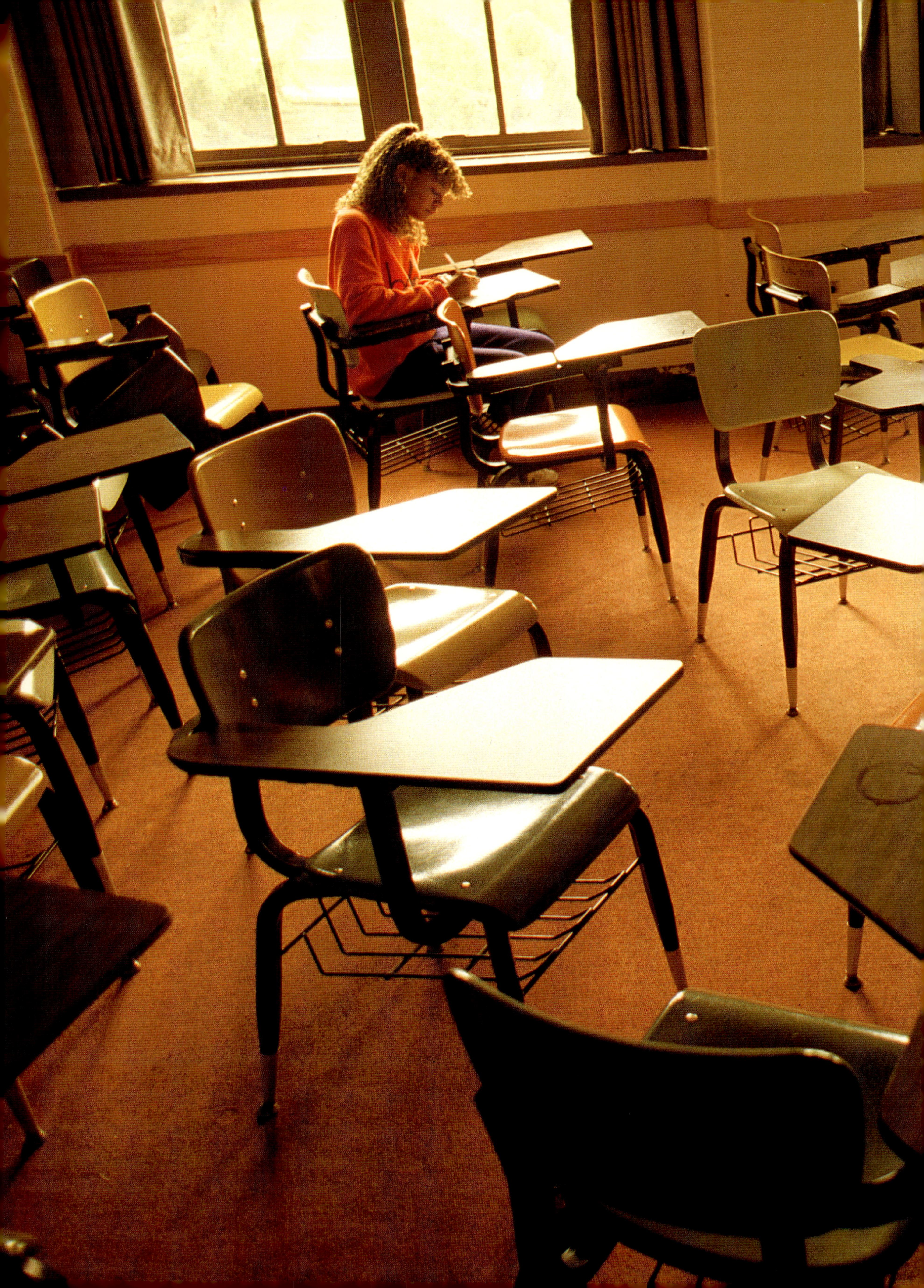

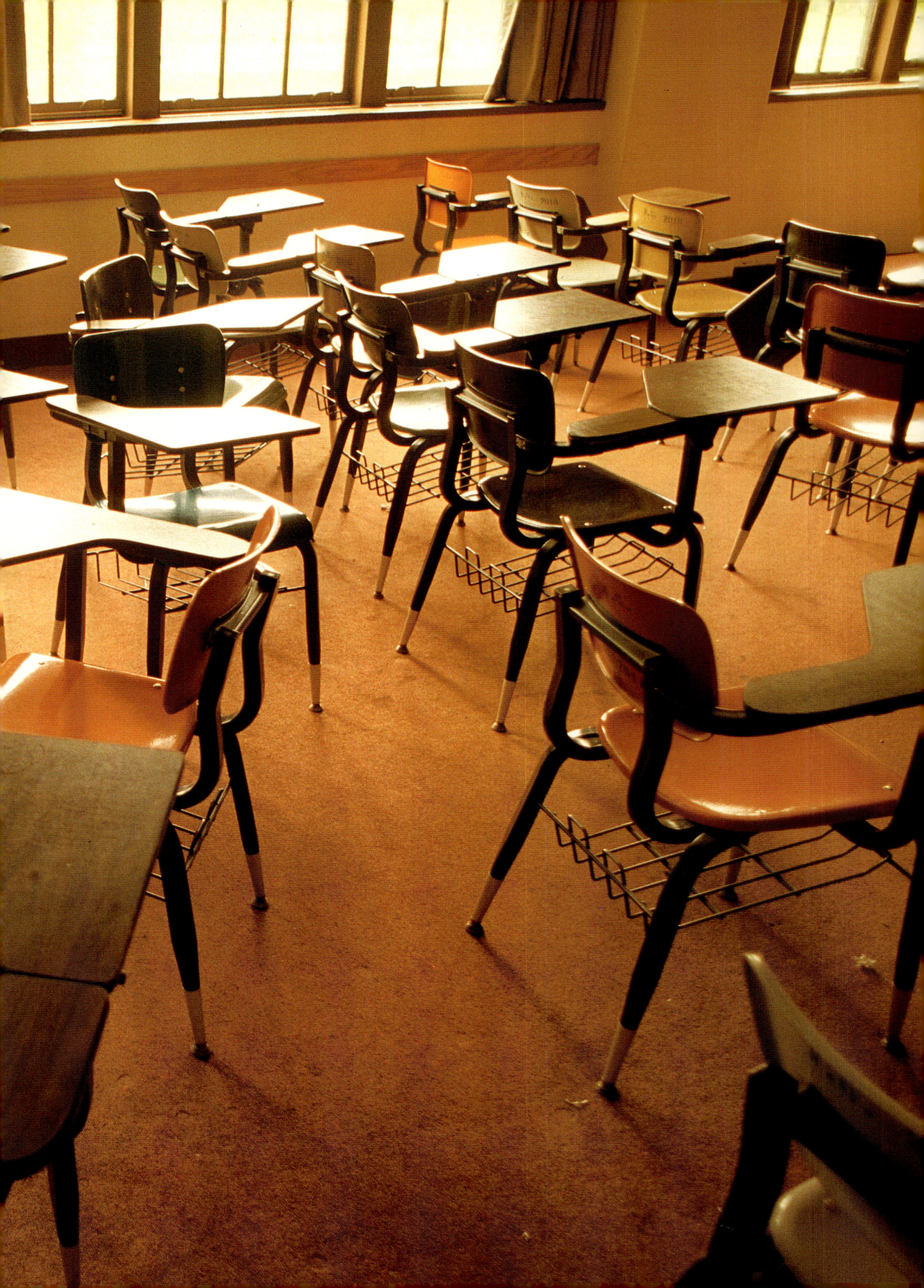

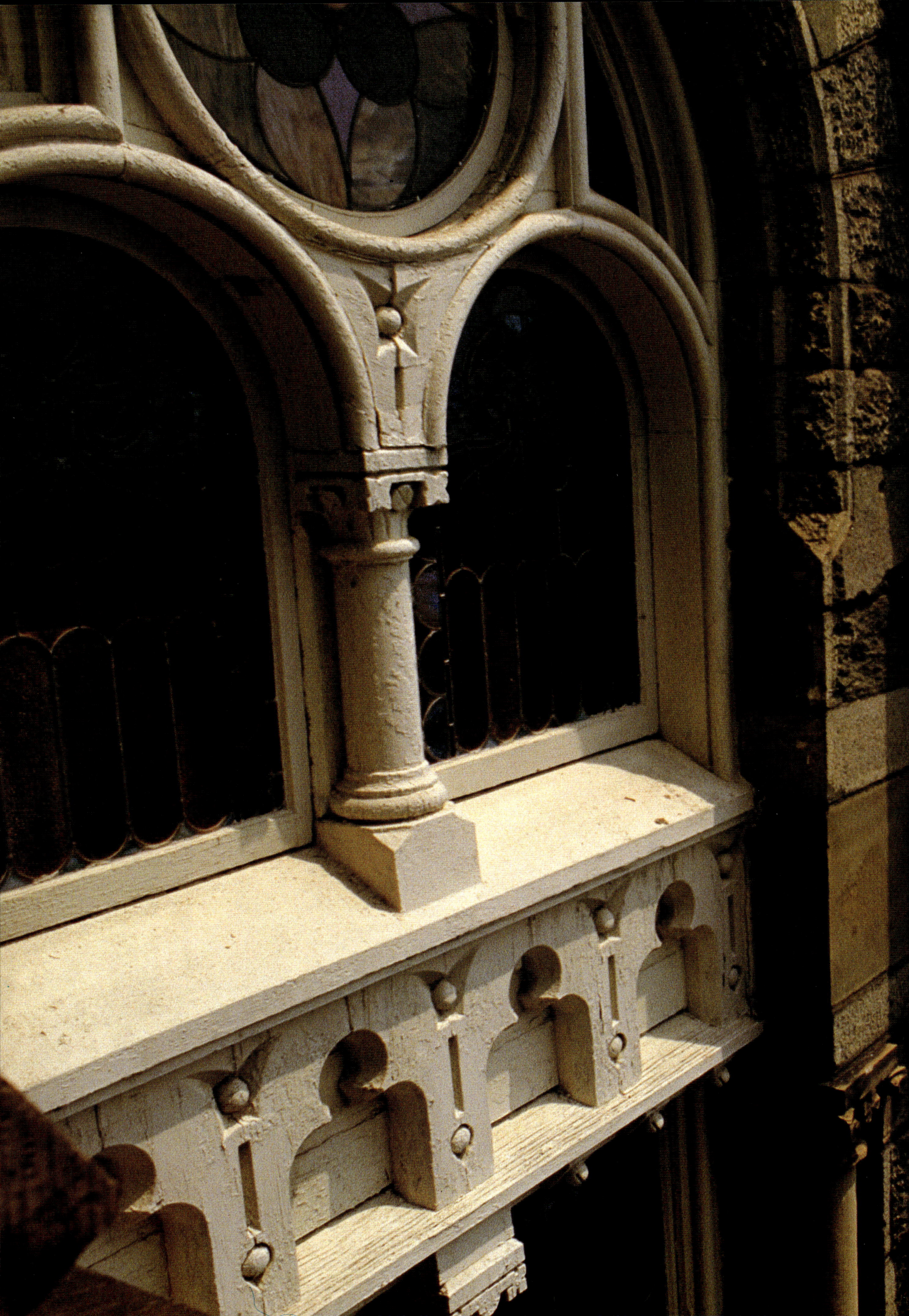

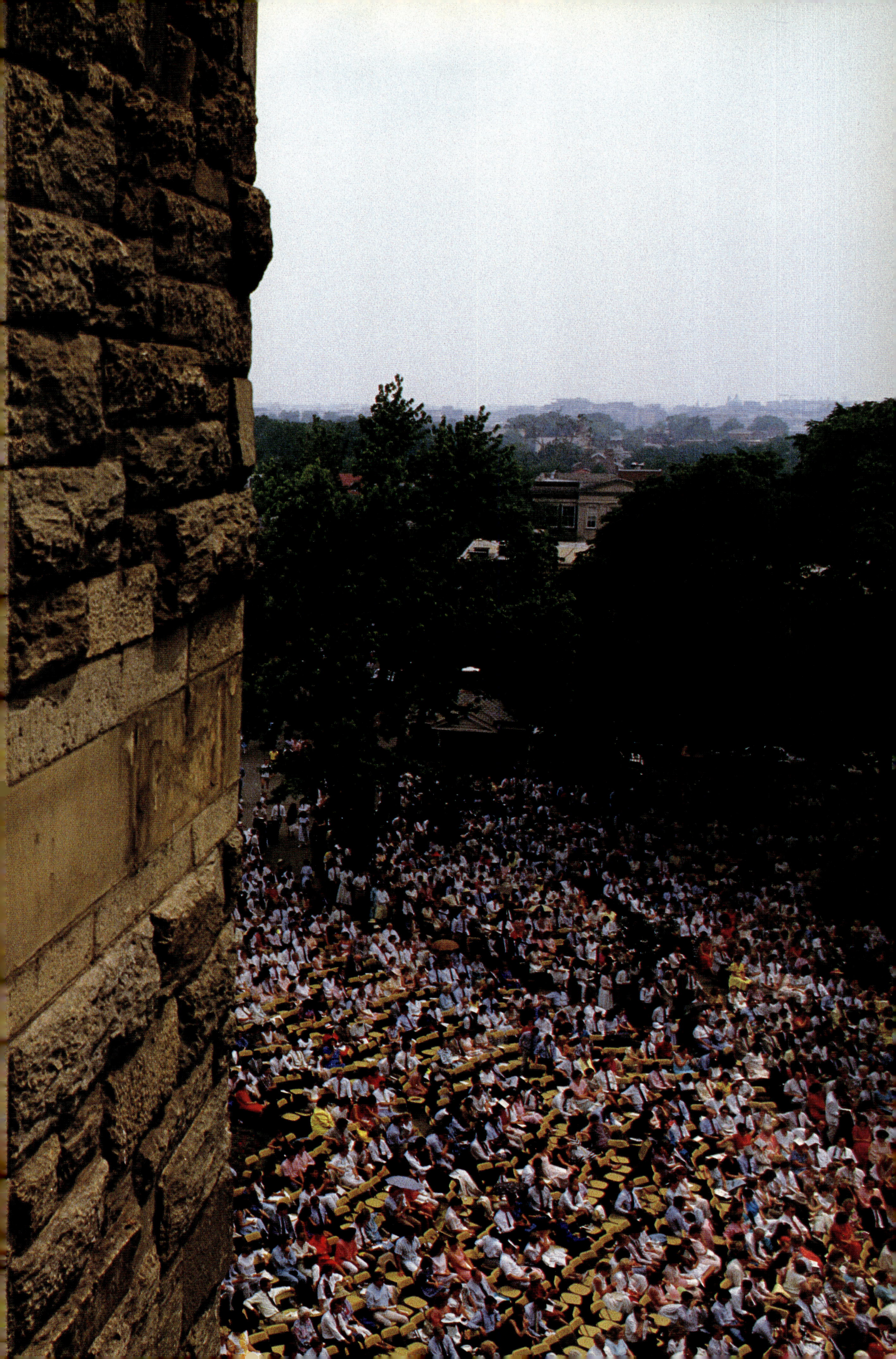

dozen hospitals and as many courtrooms, great and little, the learning of Georgetown reaches the poor, the orphan, the widow and the sick. The University should not take credit for what its faculty, students or alumni do, but it can take credit for their gathering and for their heightened skills.

All rivers draw down from deep in the land. Beyond our city lies a nation, and for it our service is larger. In classrooms, laboratories and libraries, we are continually remaking the American Republic. Term after term, as the energy and enthusiasm of the young bang into the learning and experience of the faculty, we are engaged in a Whiteheadian process that keeps this nation restless and alive and indeed, despite her centuries, young. We elders cannot know this future, even though we labor in the minds and hearts of the young to make it happen, to give it shape. Yet we are surely a part of its shaping, we who use the present to keep the past and at the same time ready the future.

Old houses grow into the land that holds them. Georgetown's river and hill and city explain much of what Carroll's "little academy" has become over two centuries. The three realities of our site are contradictory. River and hill tug against each other, and both are altered by the crushing demands a

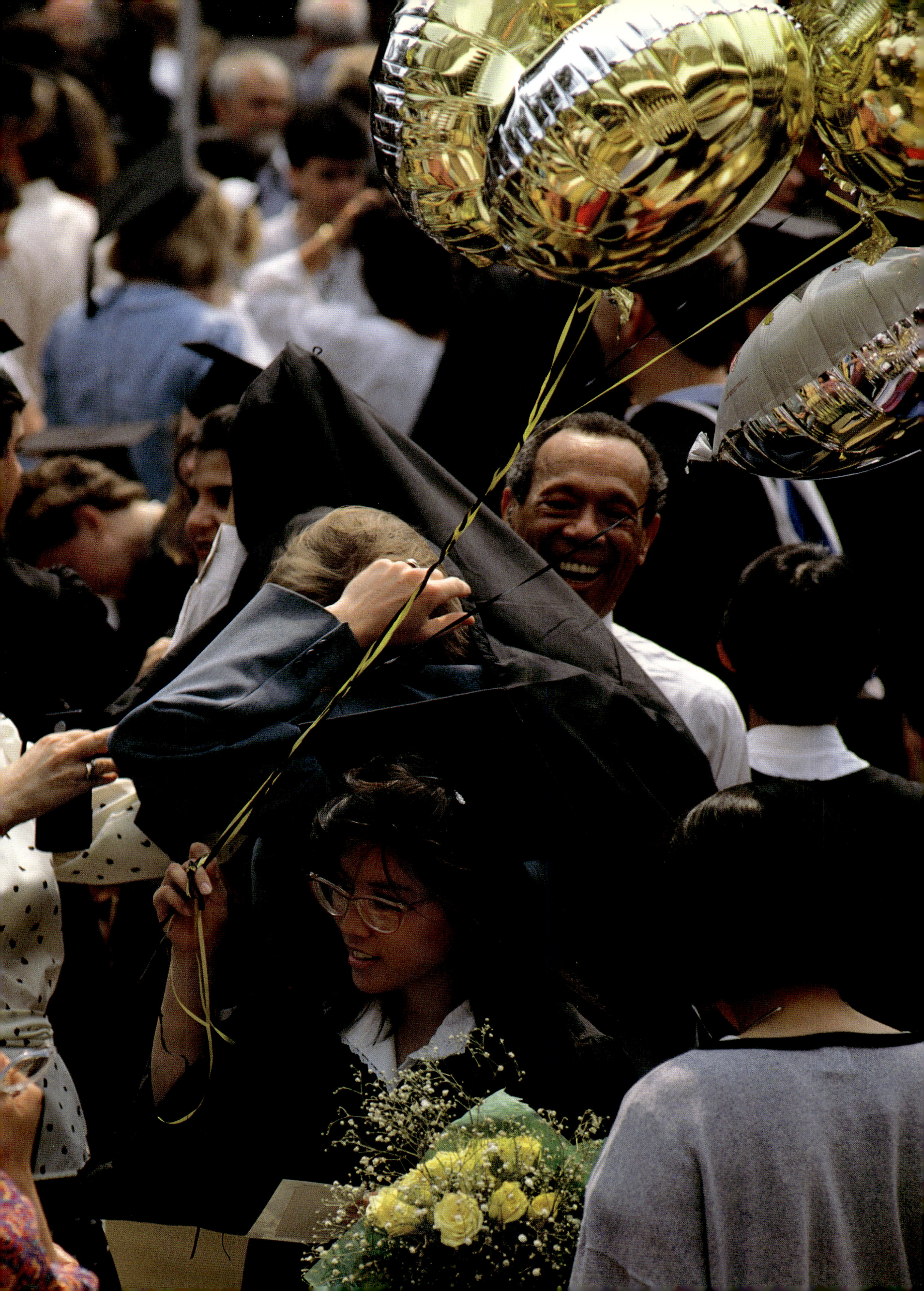

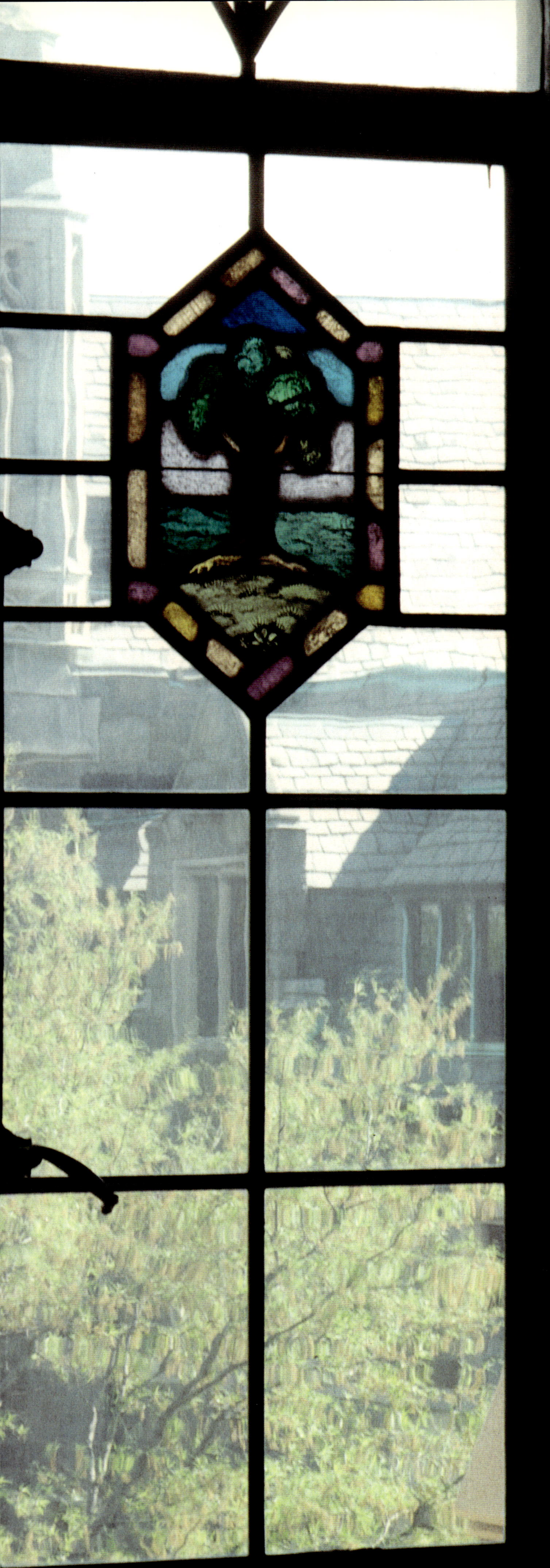

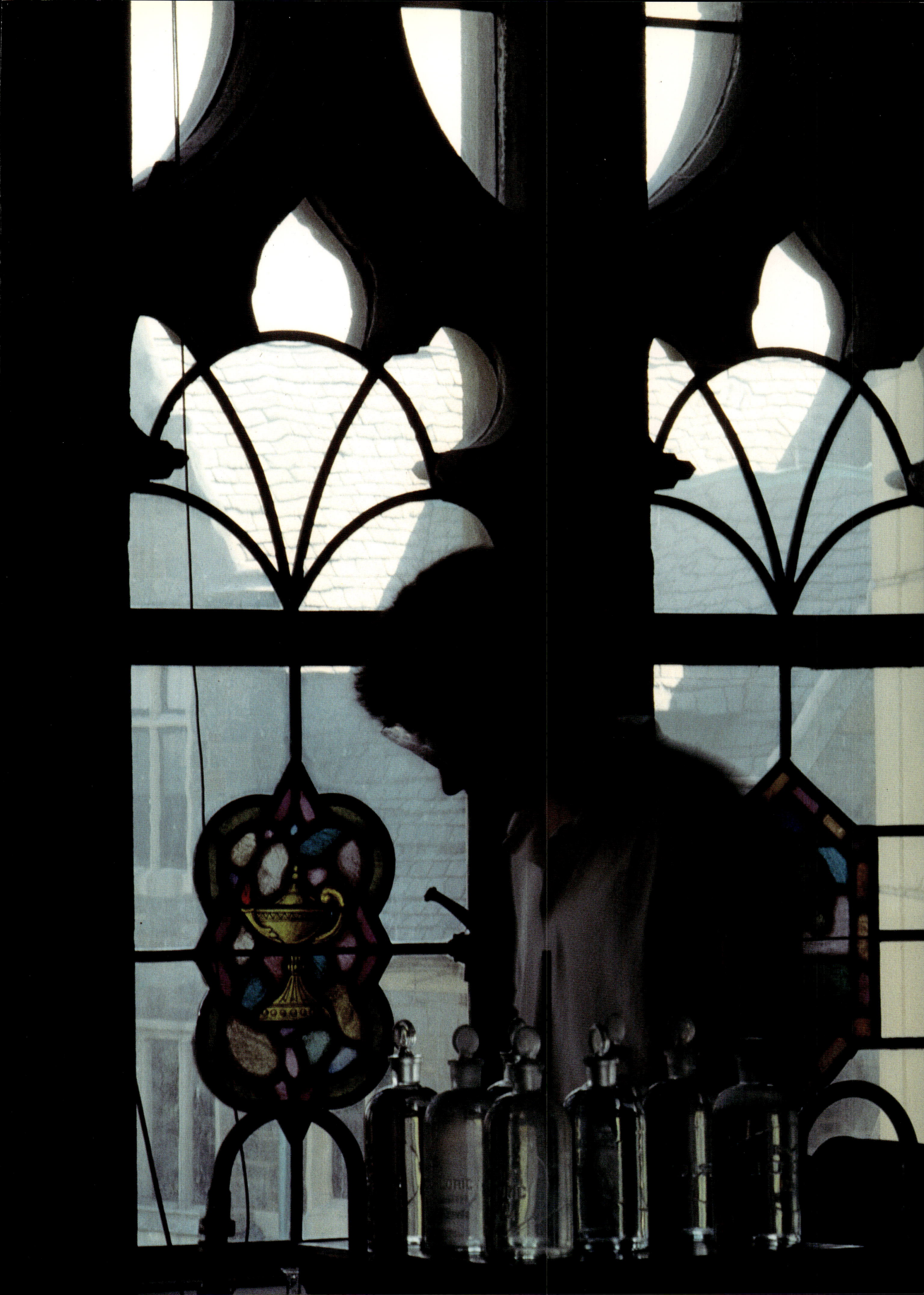

THE OLD RÉGIME AND THE FRENCH REVOLUTION
LIBRARY OF HISTORY
ALEXIS DE TOCQUEVILLE

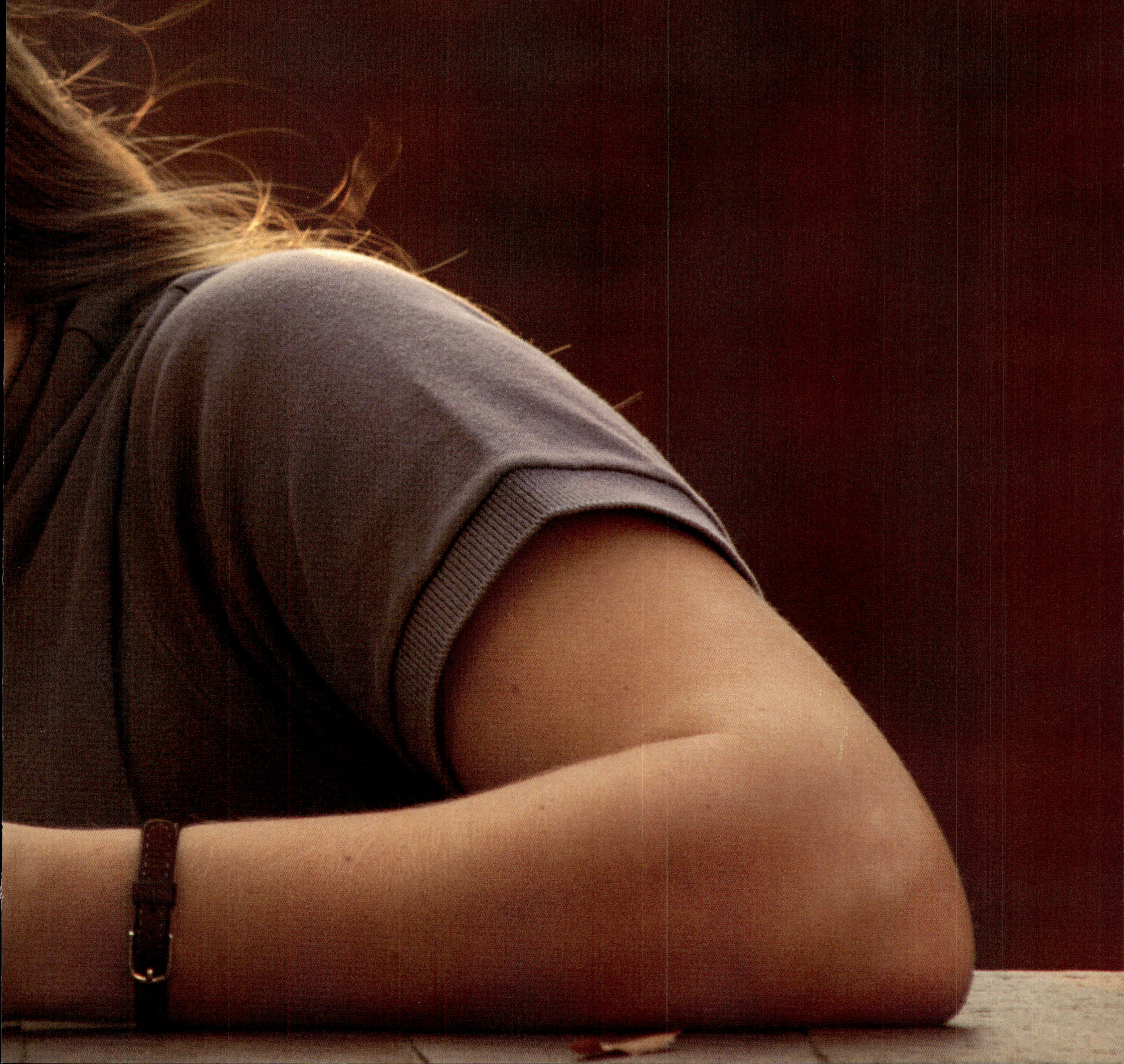

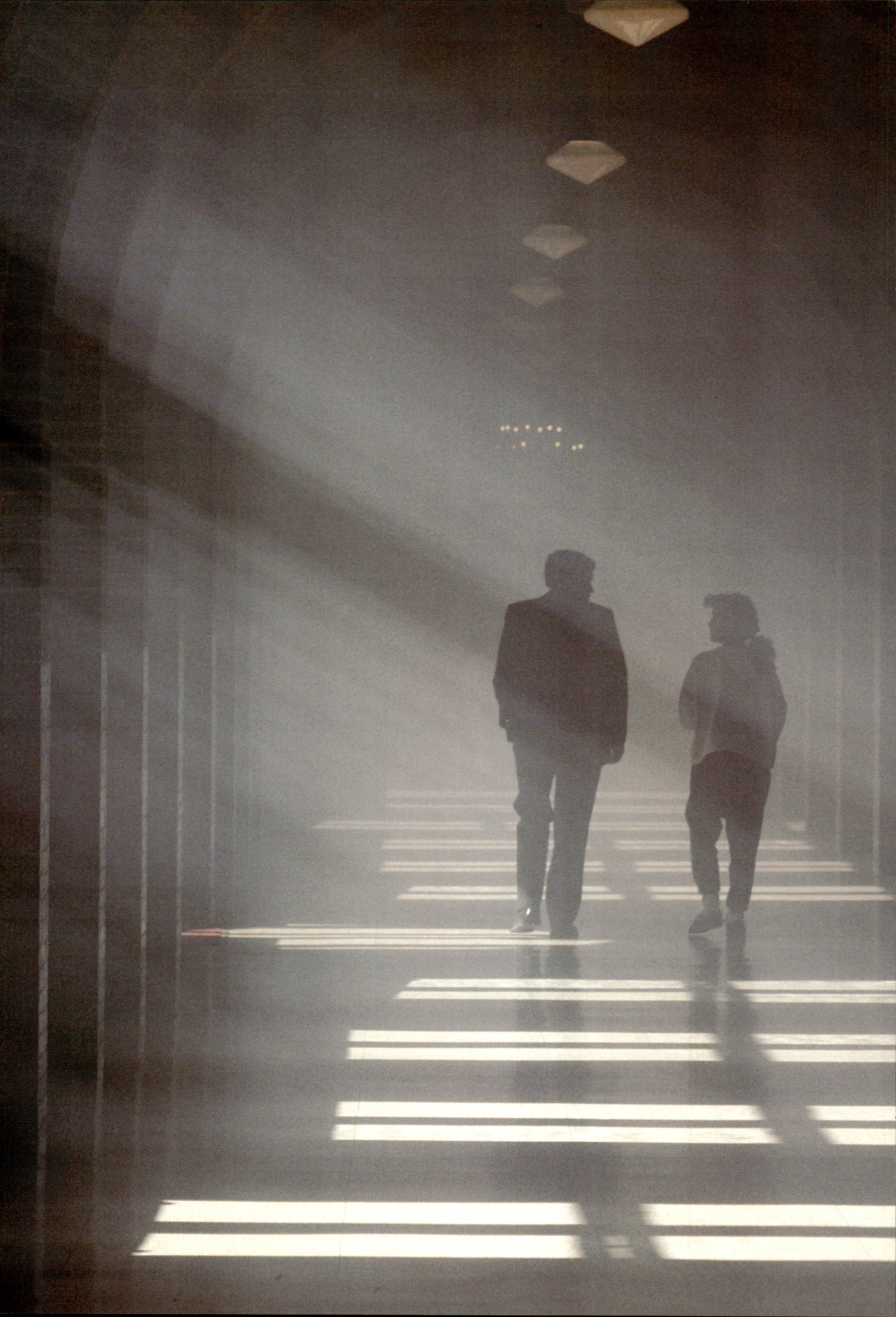

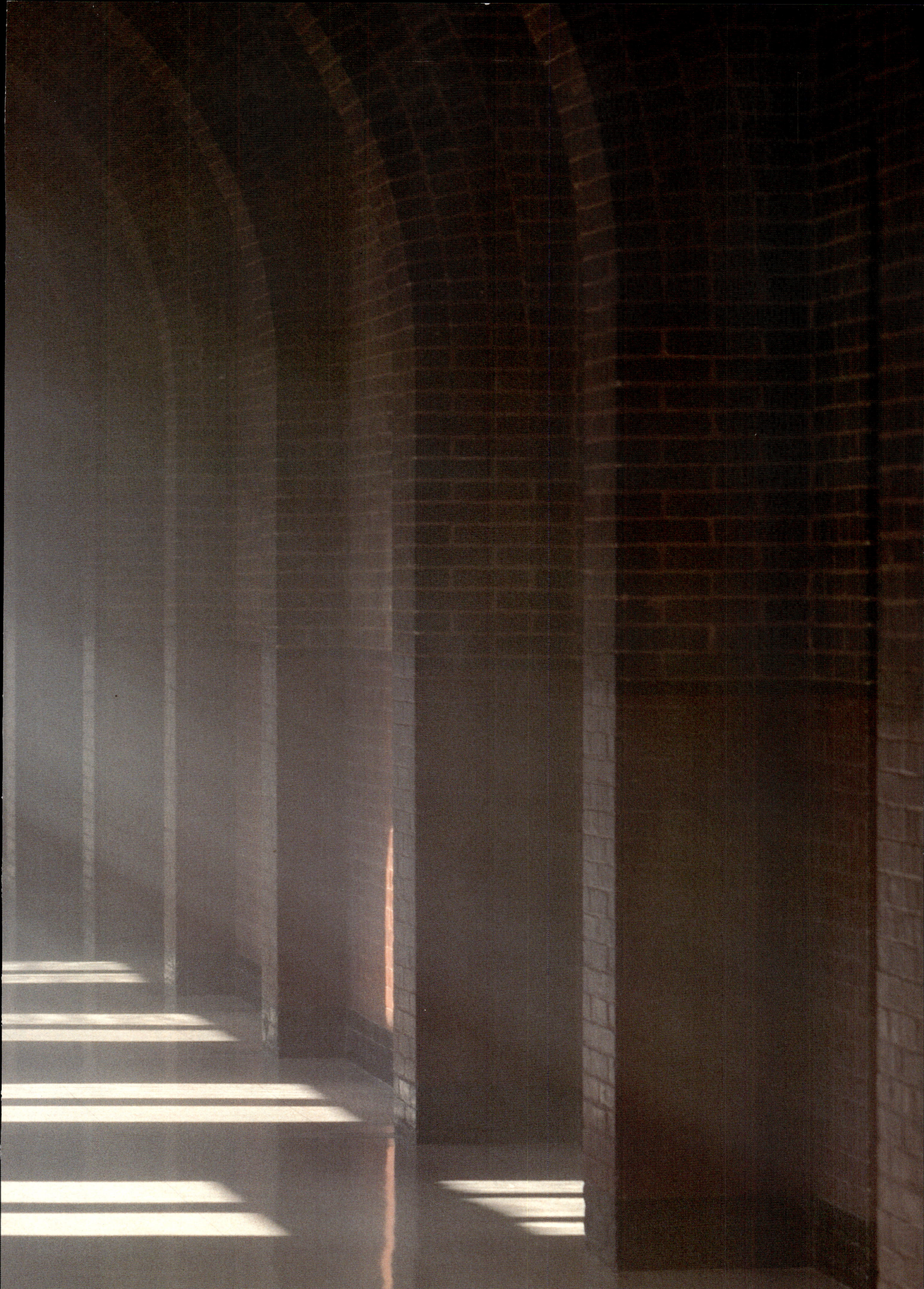

great city can make. How well the University balances all three depends on the time and on our skill. One thing is sure, perfect balance is ever the goal we never will reach.

The flow of our Bicentennial has tossed up hundreds of old photos and sketches, old buildings now gone, and groups with Greek names. Some classical hybrids, like the raunchy cheer "Hoya Saxa!" have lasted. We smile at the formal photographs, at the boatered, celluloid-collared young in stiff poses. We ache for the vulnerability of young faces over gray, blue or khaki uniforms. We can laugh at the artfully grouped teams, their players draped over each other like heaped teddy bears. We want to say, "how different they were." But as we look closer, our memories tell us that the differences are mostly in poses and clothes. These young faces in their day were one-half of our great experiment; the other half, the faculty, seems to have changed less, despite our shedding of cassocks and flowing beards. River and rock contrast – the experiment abides.

Undergraduate teaching, with its dream of making citizens for the City of Man and the City of God, has always been first in Georgetown's time and heart. For two centuries on this good ground the faculty has labored to help young men, and for the last thirty years young women, to achieve themselves as

[citizens]

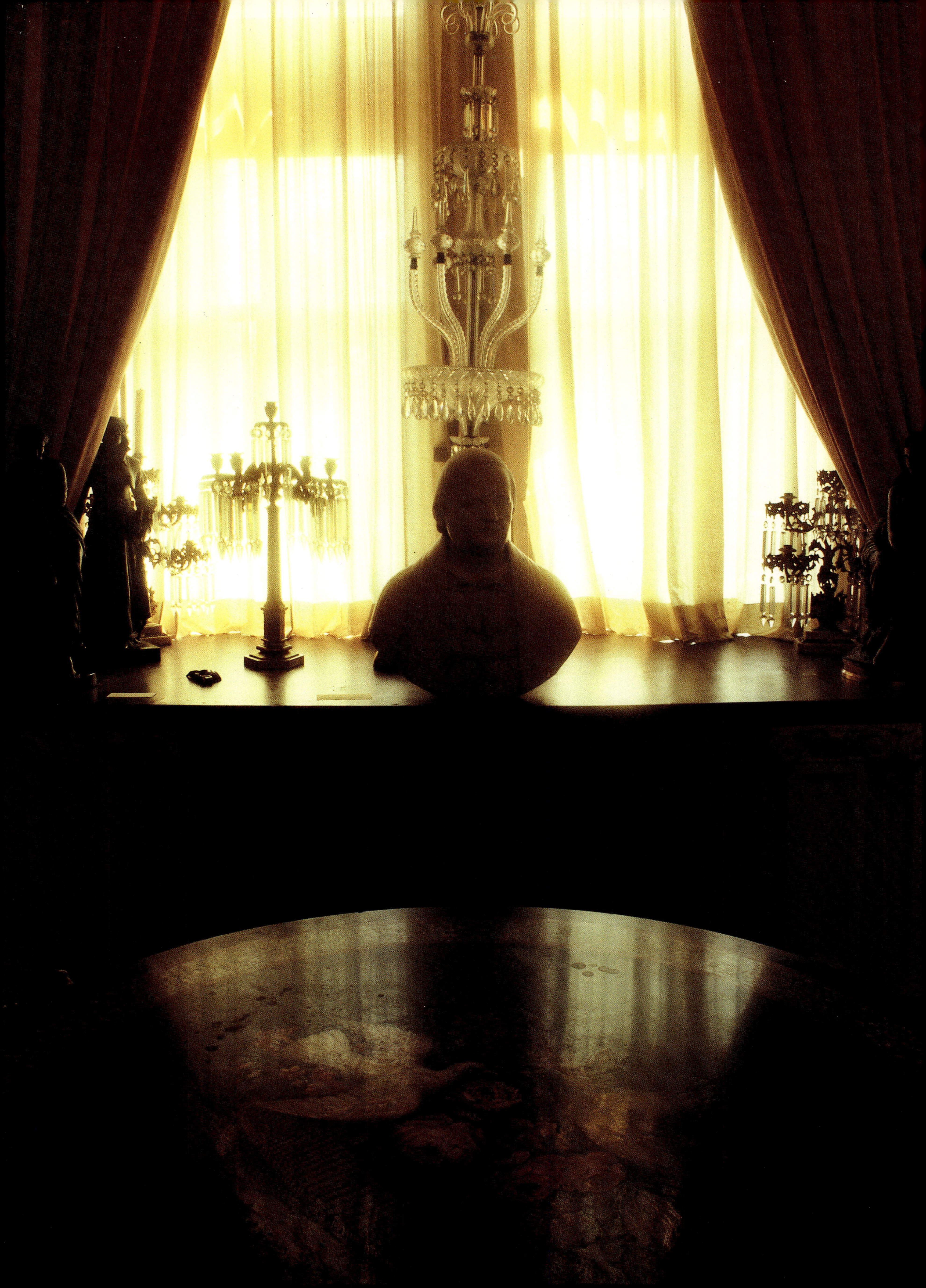

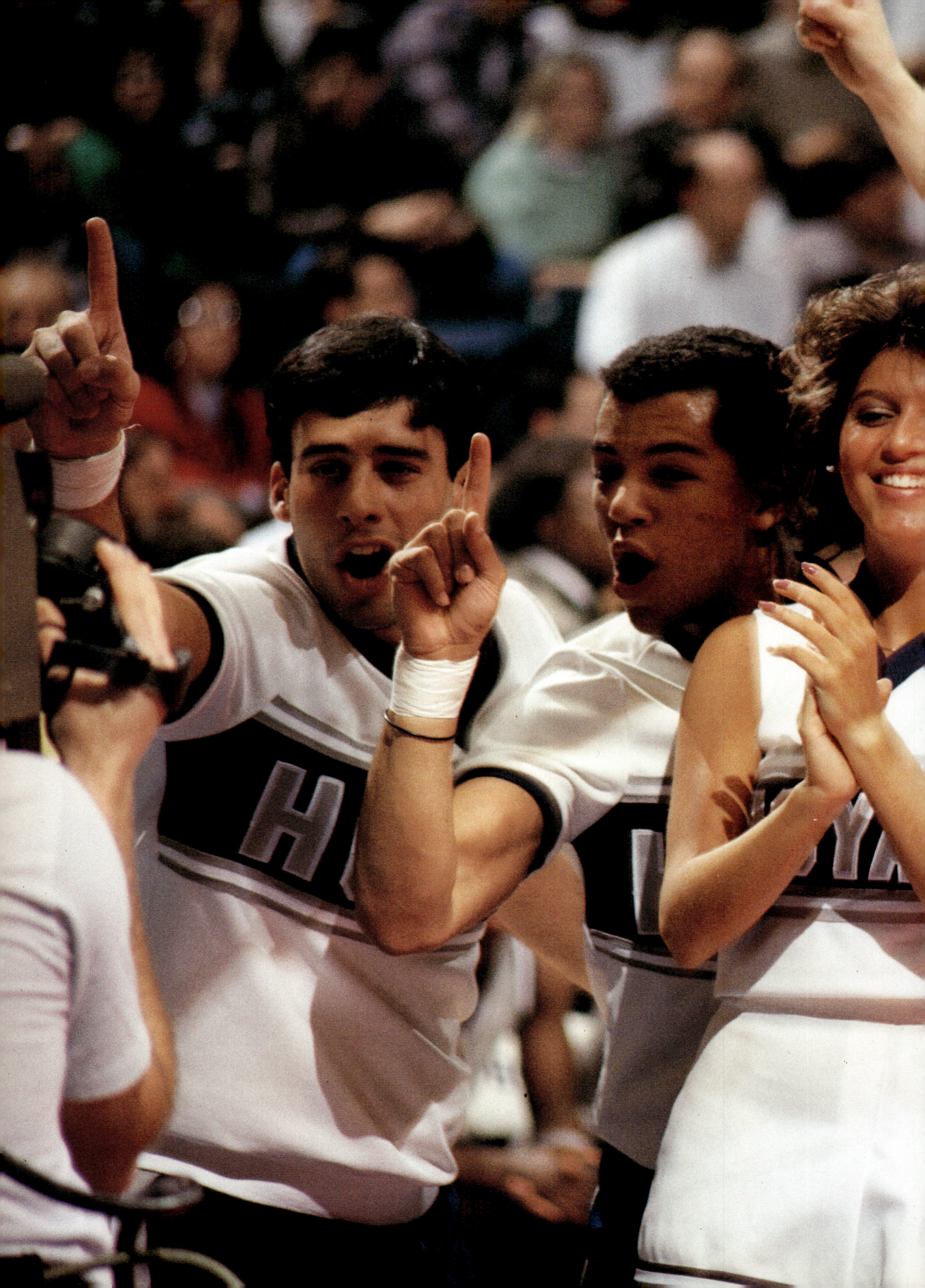

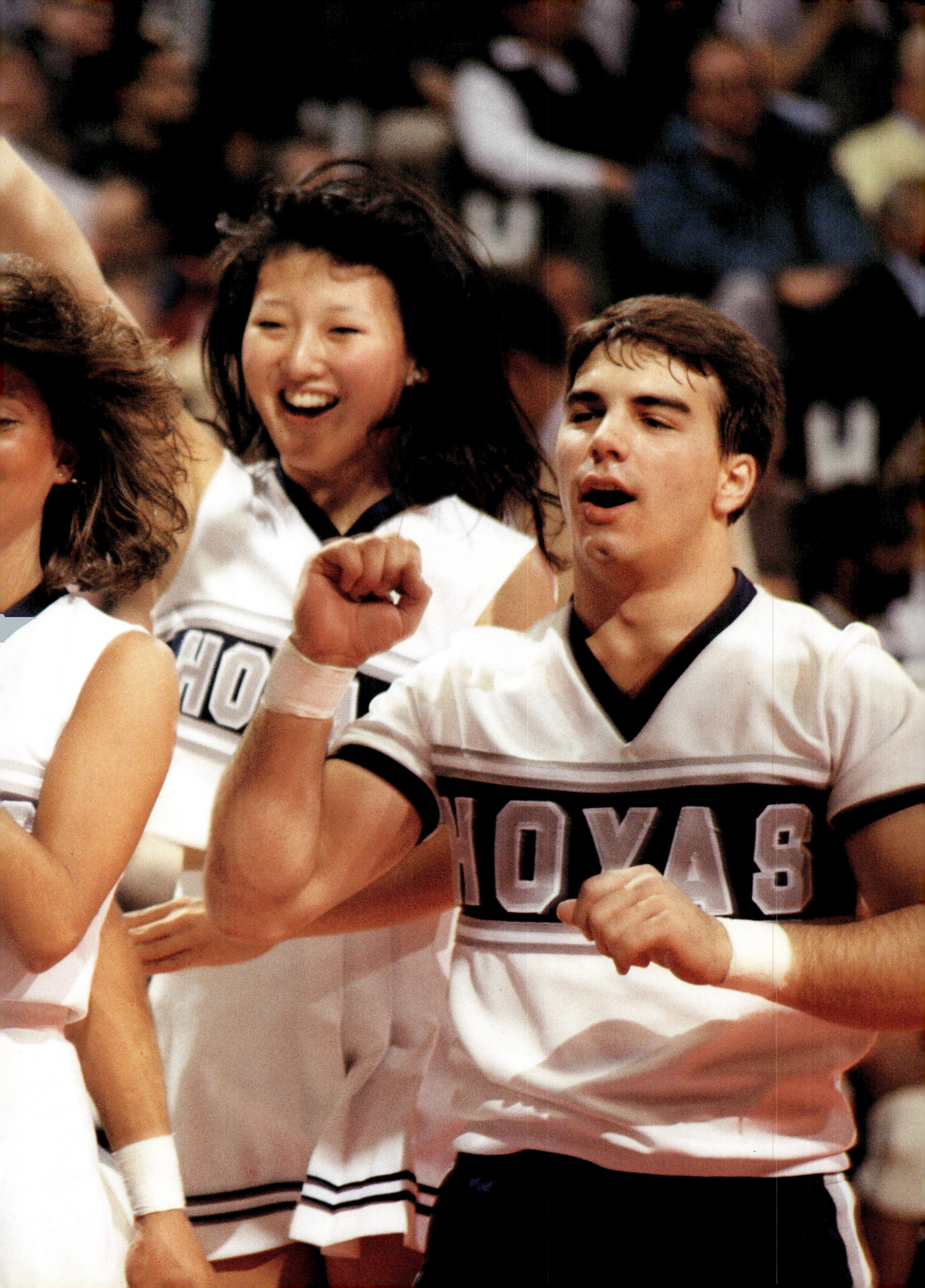
HOYAS

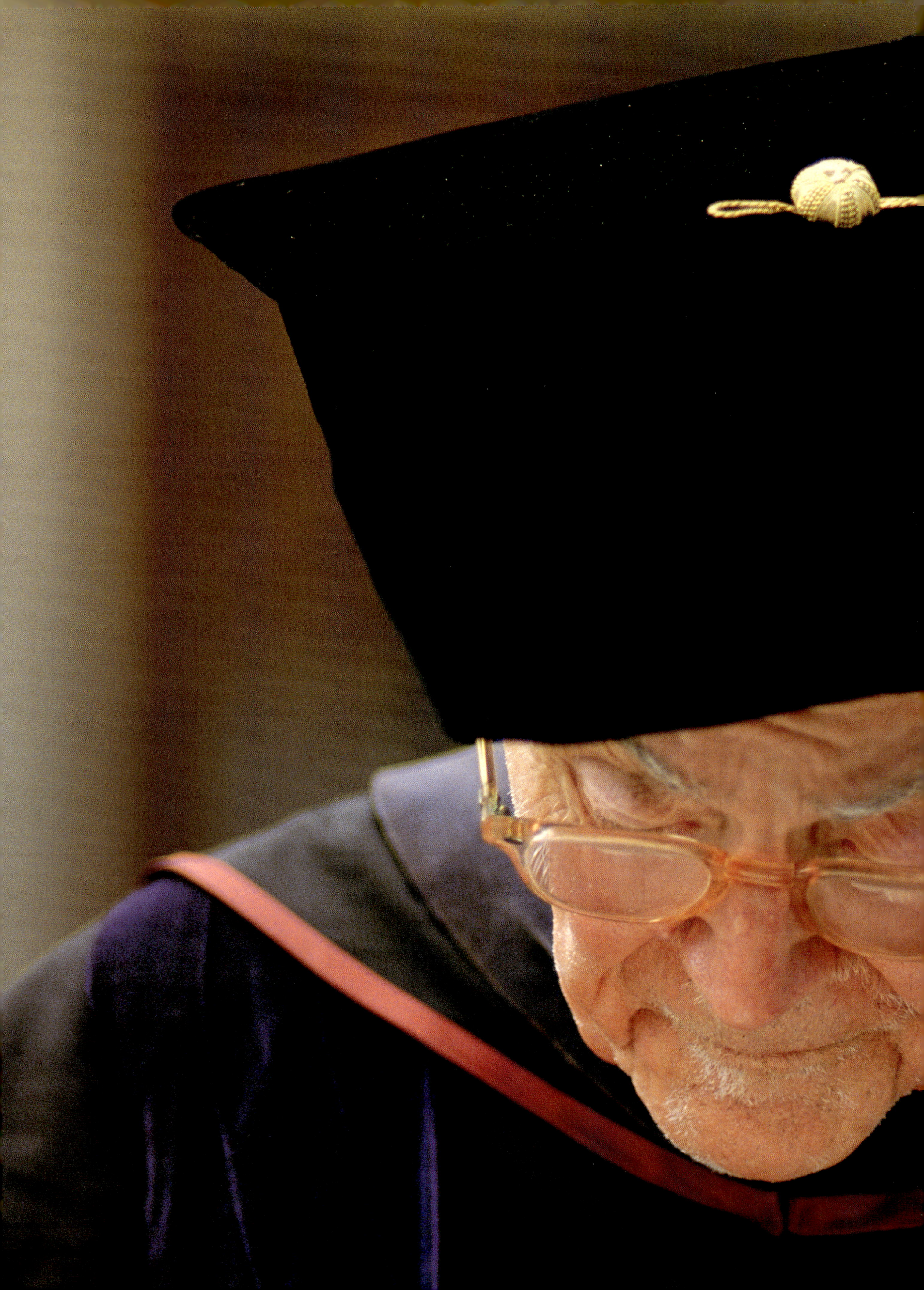

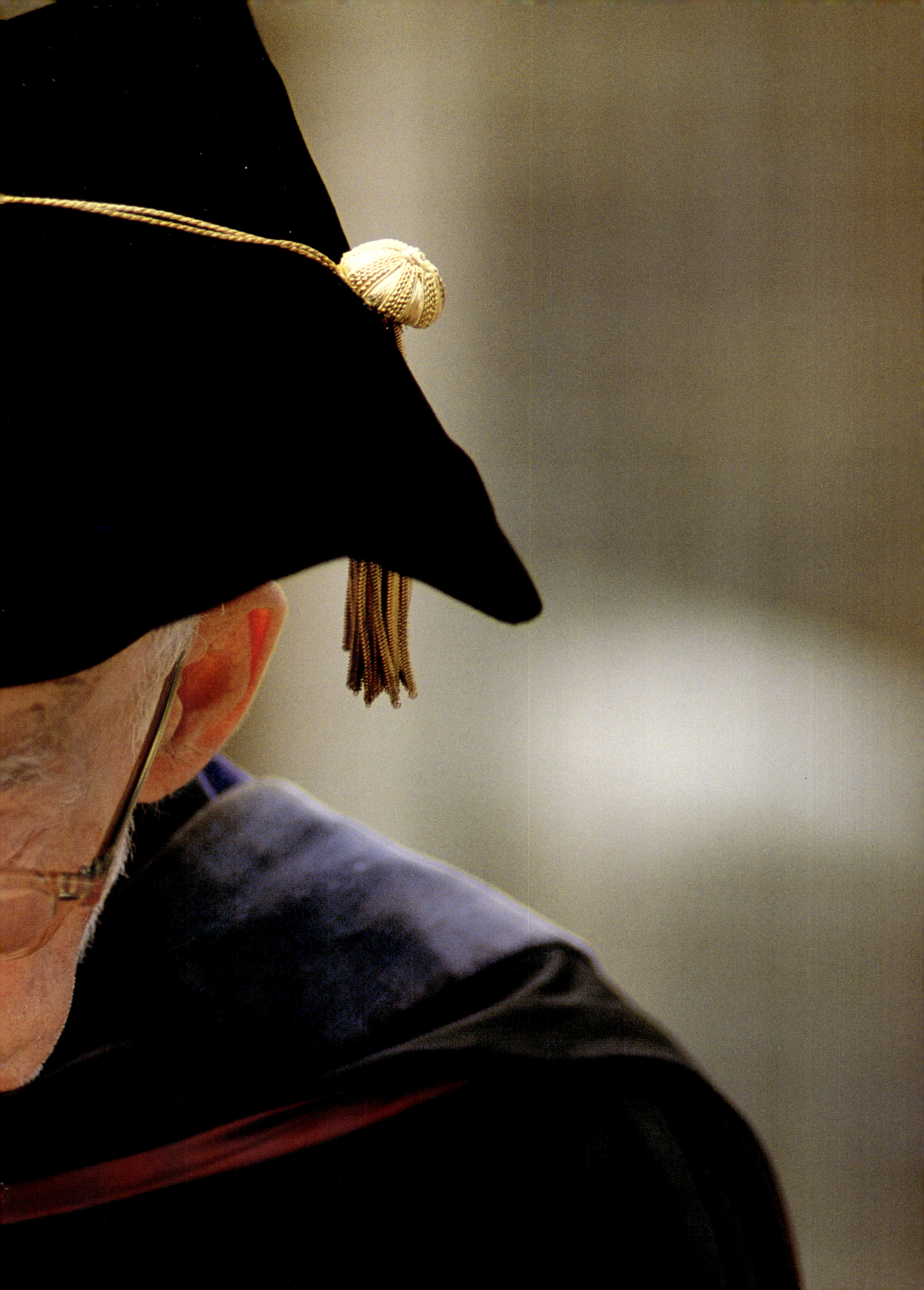

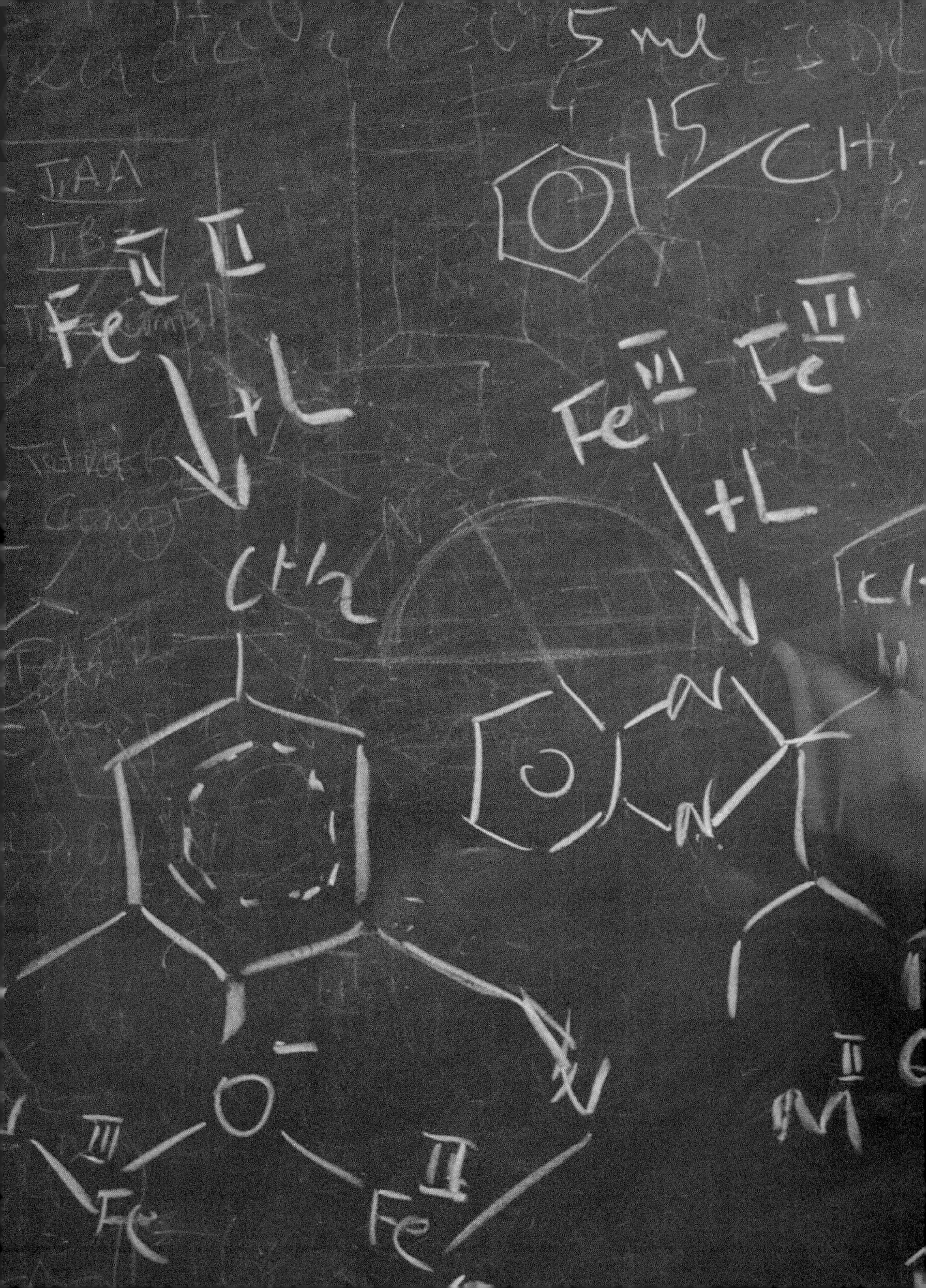

5 ml
15
CH3
Fe II III
+L
Fe III
Fe III
+L
CH2
N
N
N
O
III
Fe
II
Fe
II
M

NEt$_3$

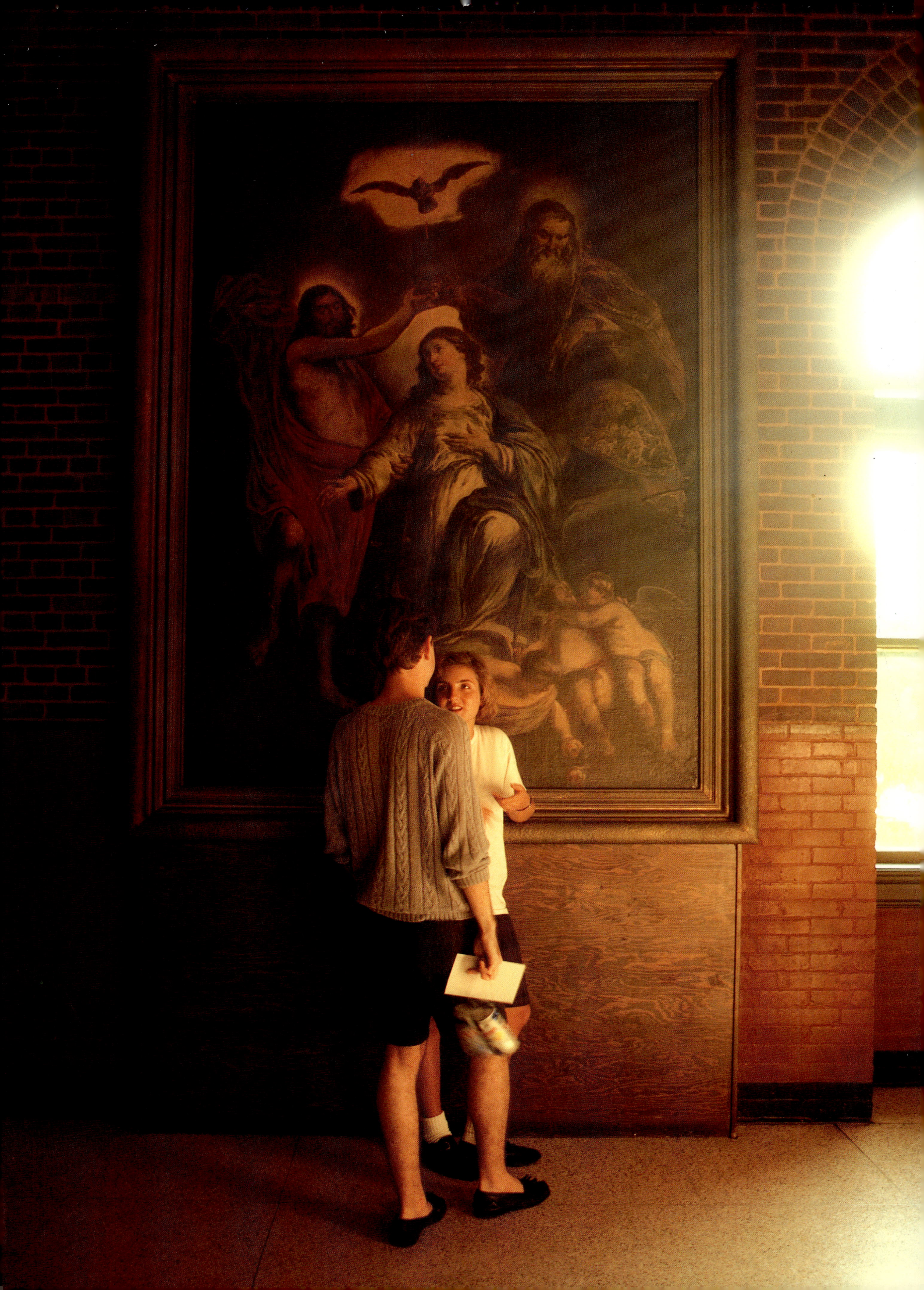

citizens, husbands and wives, parents and as friends. "Liberal education" has always had those aims and only those. At times we have been wrested out of our sense of ourselves by wars and depressions, by the will-o-the-wisps of intellectual fashion, by the grim careerism of a consumer society. Thus the river eddies, but the hill has made sure that we have never bowed to either of two heresies – that the bachelor's degree is for making a living rather than for life itself, or that one can debase the arts and sciences to make them "value free." Neither fallacy has ever clouded the renaissance Jesuit vision that everything human, as well as the nature in which mankind sits, is filled with the laboring presence of God and thus worth the struggle to enjoy, understand and celebrate.

Before its first century was out, Georgetown began teaching law and medicine. Much to their loss, these two professional schools are today tugged and pulled by bodies of practitioners, organized and arrogant, and vastly careless of the aims and the rhythms of a university – above all of one that believes in God. In the 20th century, far more like river than rock, it is harder than ever to urge the claims of service over gain, of understanding over usefulness and above all of freedom over conformity. Georgetown labors to edit a national journal of

[legal]

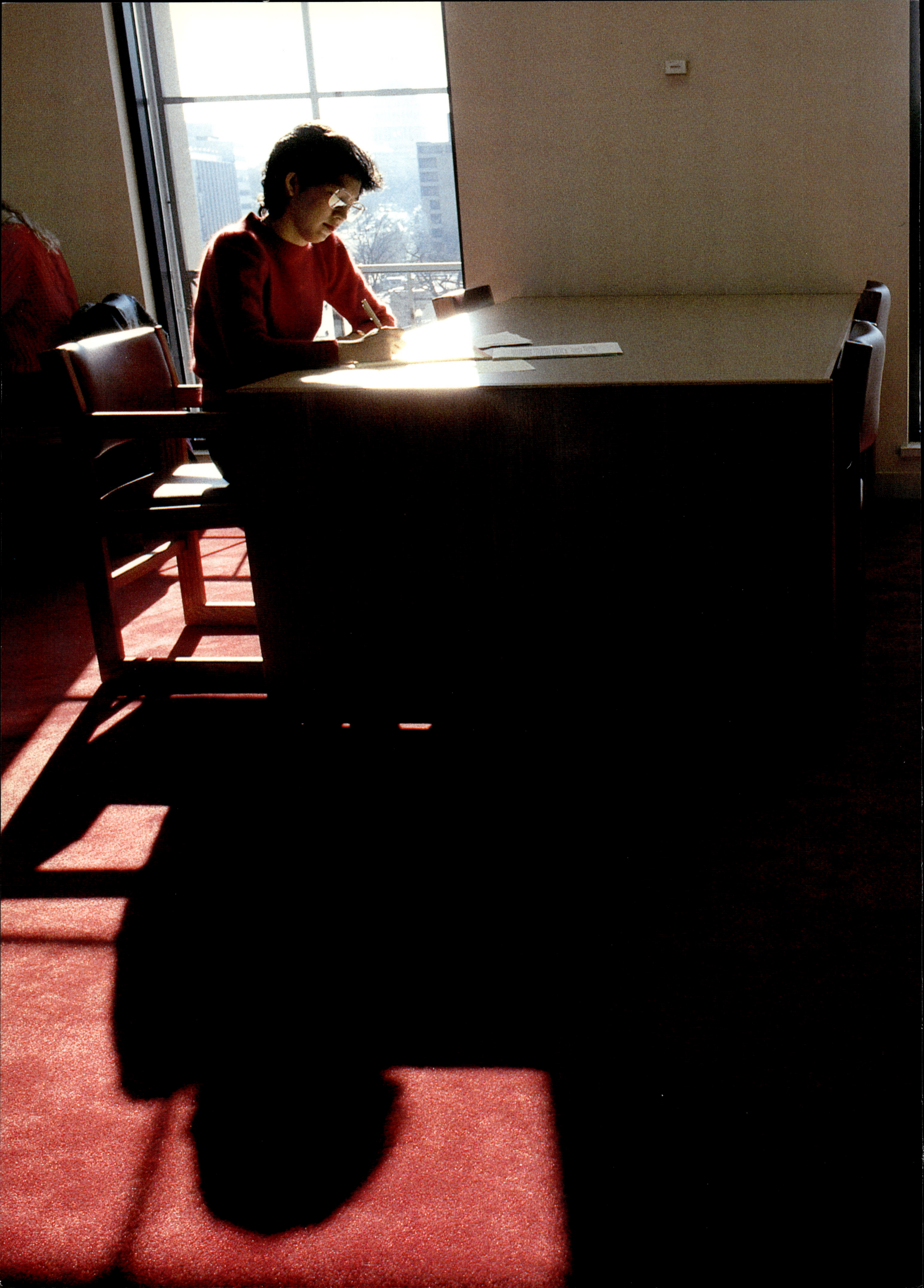

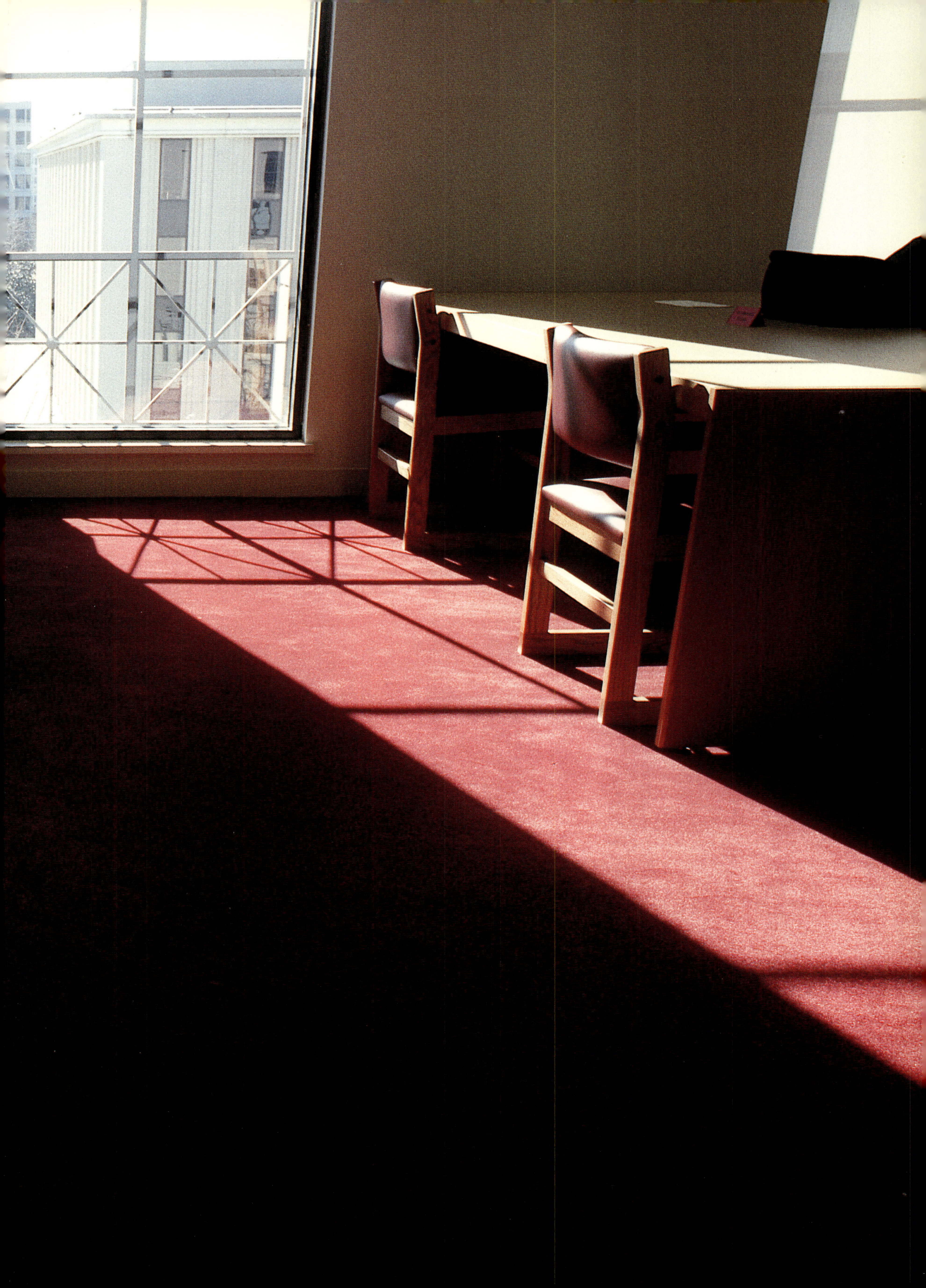

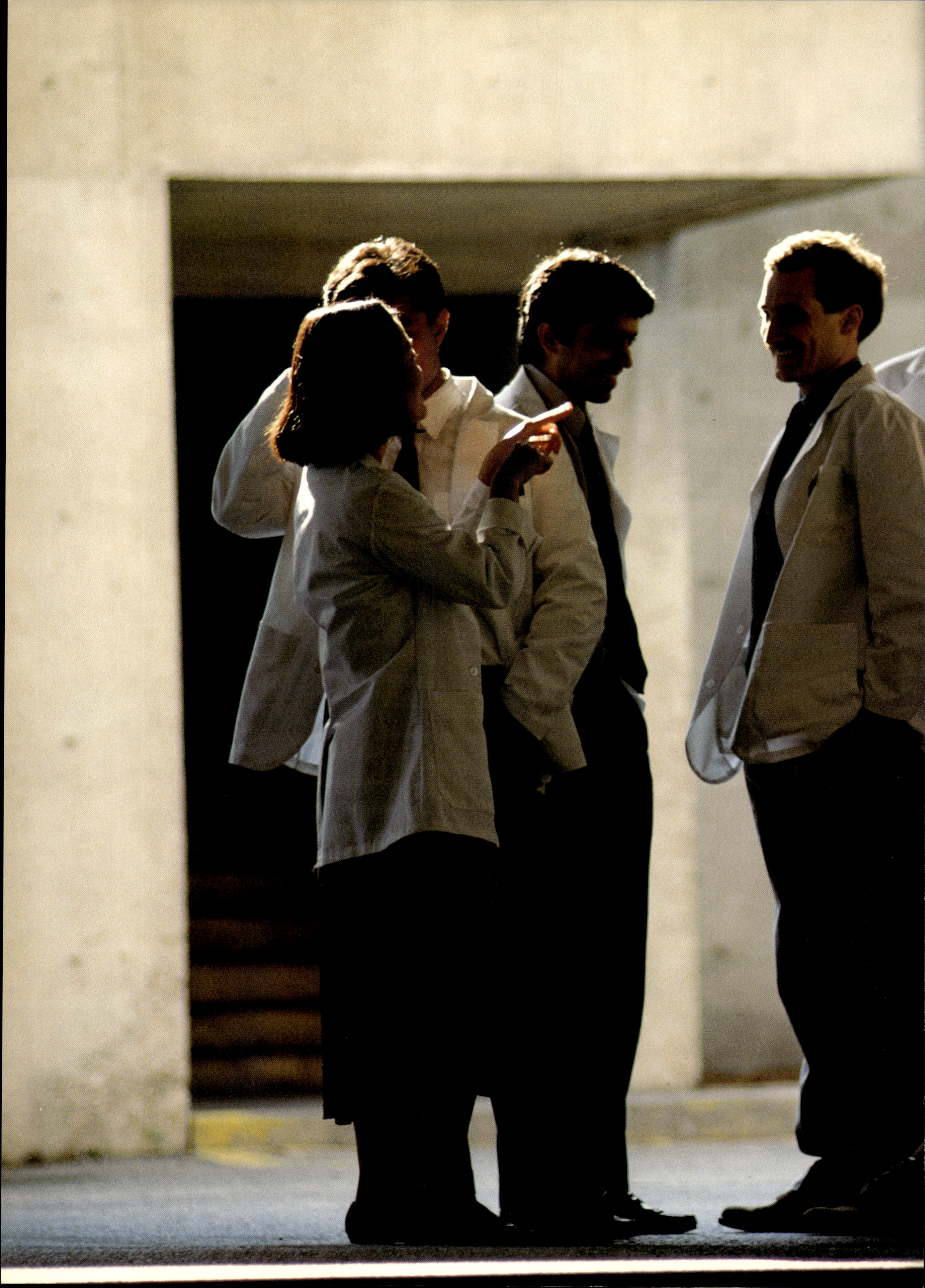

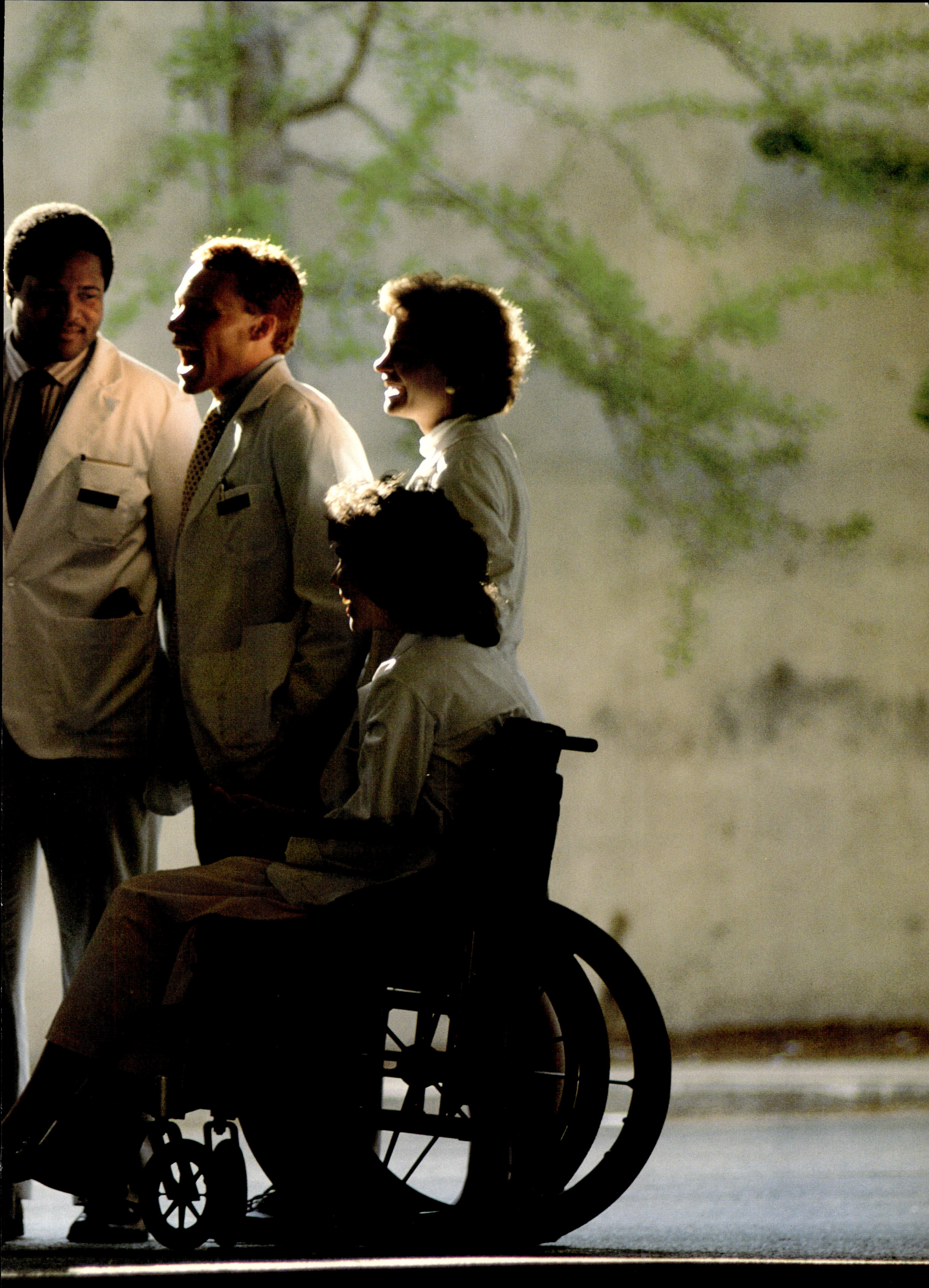

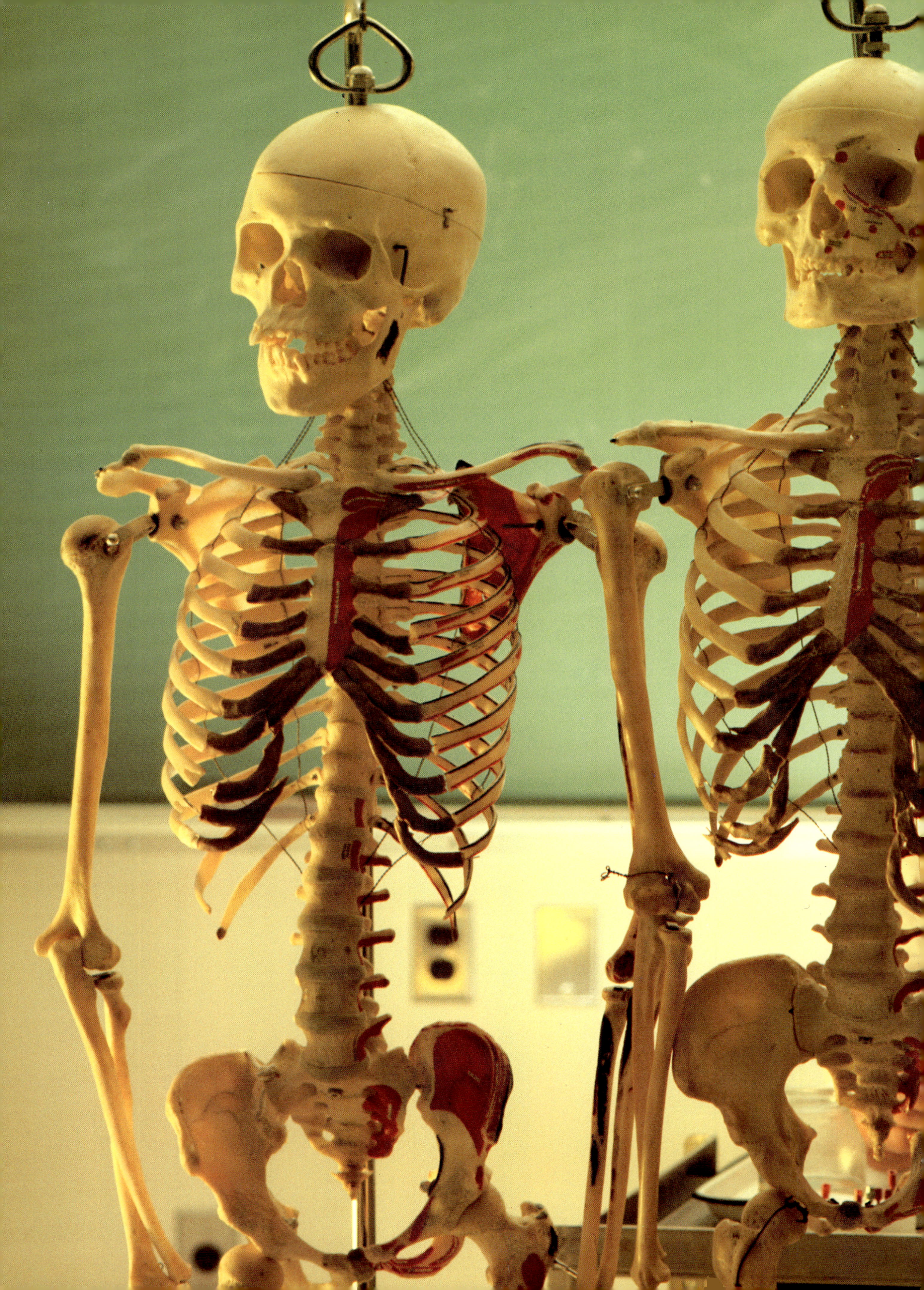

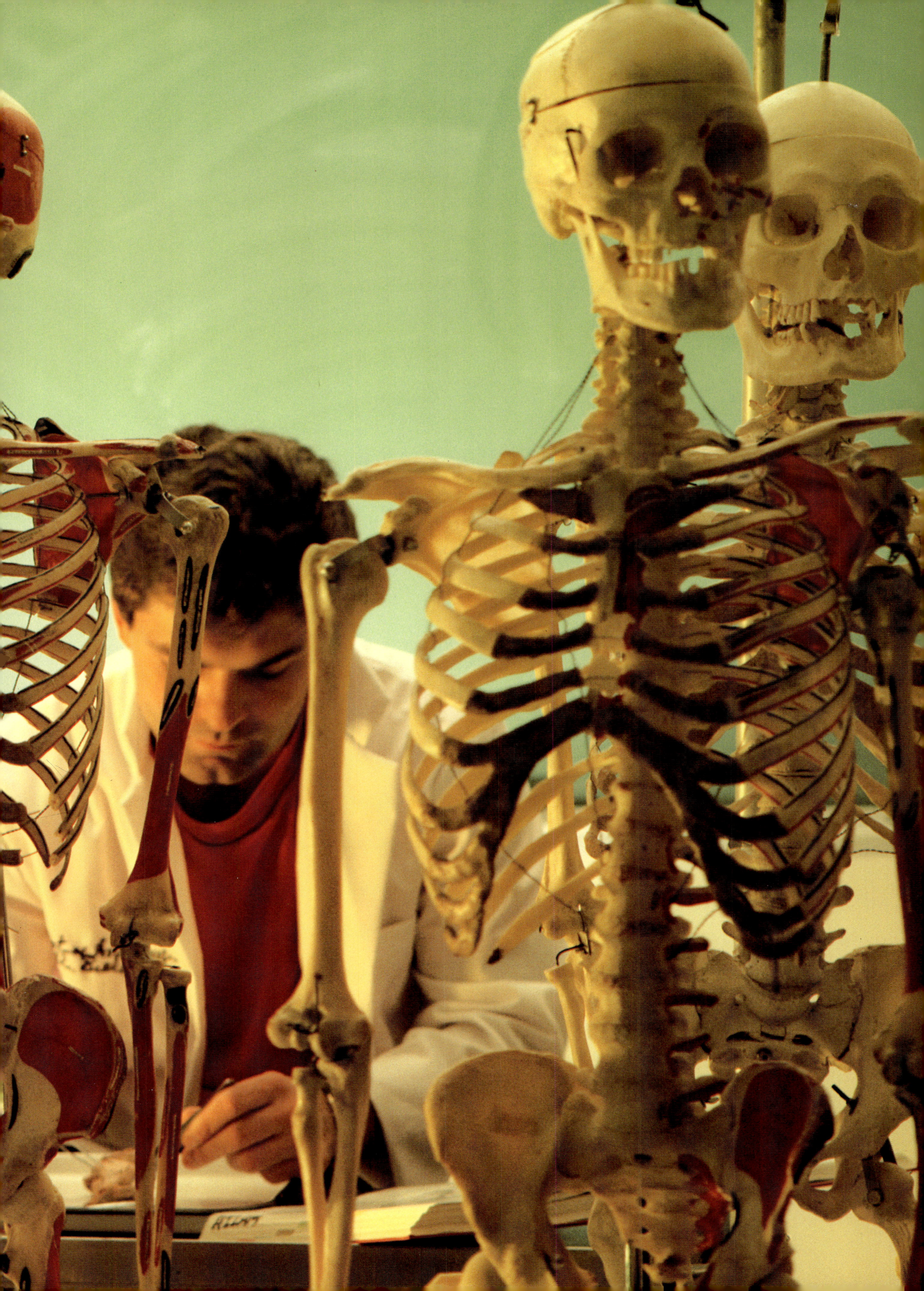

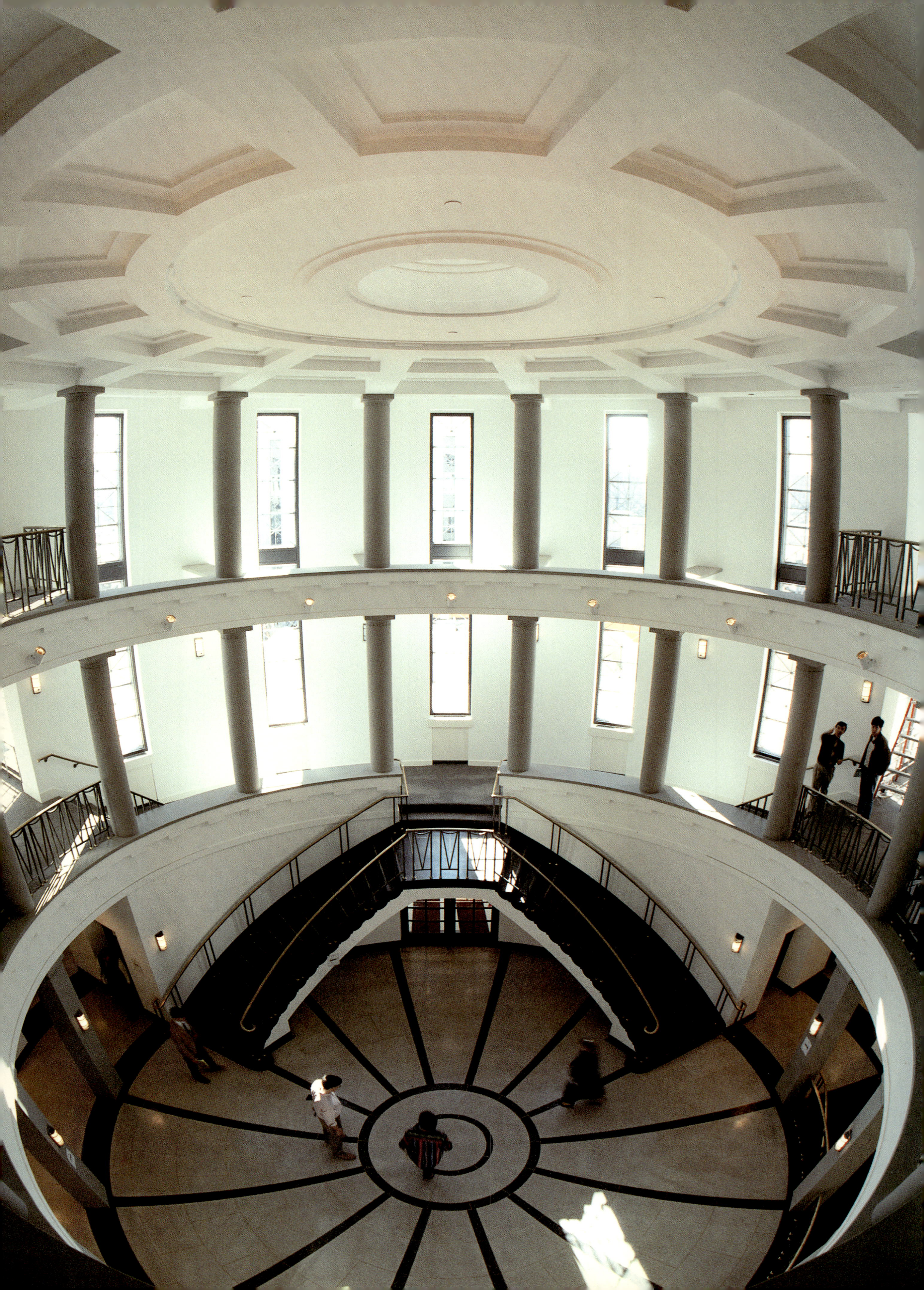

legal ethics and to support a center for bioethics. Such endeavors and a dozen like them help us keep faith with our founders and the reach of our history. A university can fight for a profession's soul as well as for its own.

The teeming city also lays on our shoulders one more burden to which Georgetown comes late. Graduate work is the newest of our offerings and the weakest. As we close our second century, strengthening doctoral studies leaps out as the first imperative for our third. Past and present success in collegiate, legal and medical training and research provide the model to make Georgetown complete its being – to add the doctoral research faculties that will make us what the nation's capital much needs, a great University.

Georgetown has another claim to permanence, our lasting universal, the Church. Here our service is less in what we say or do than in the witness of our very being. We are first a place of scholarship and thus of contemplation, the only human activity that extends from time to eternity. Contemplation is the air and native process of any good school, and at Georgetown, on our long walks, our sundrenched lawns, above all in the conversation of faculty and students, in the quiet of the library, in the still flow of studies that speak change, that contempla-

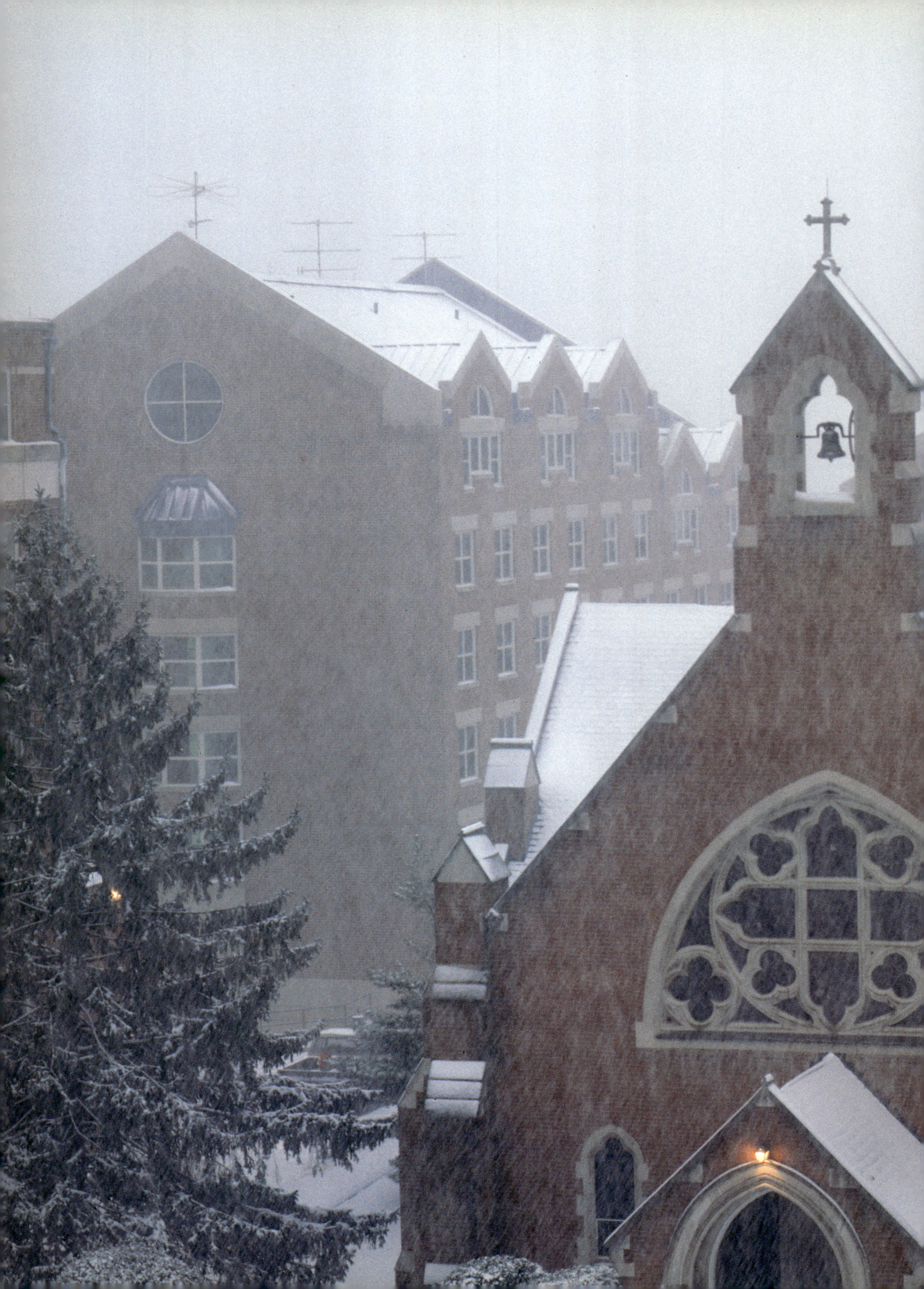

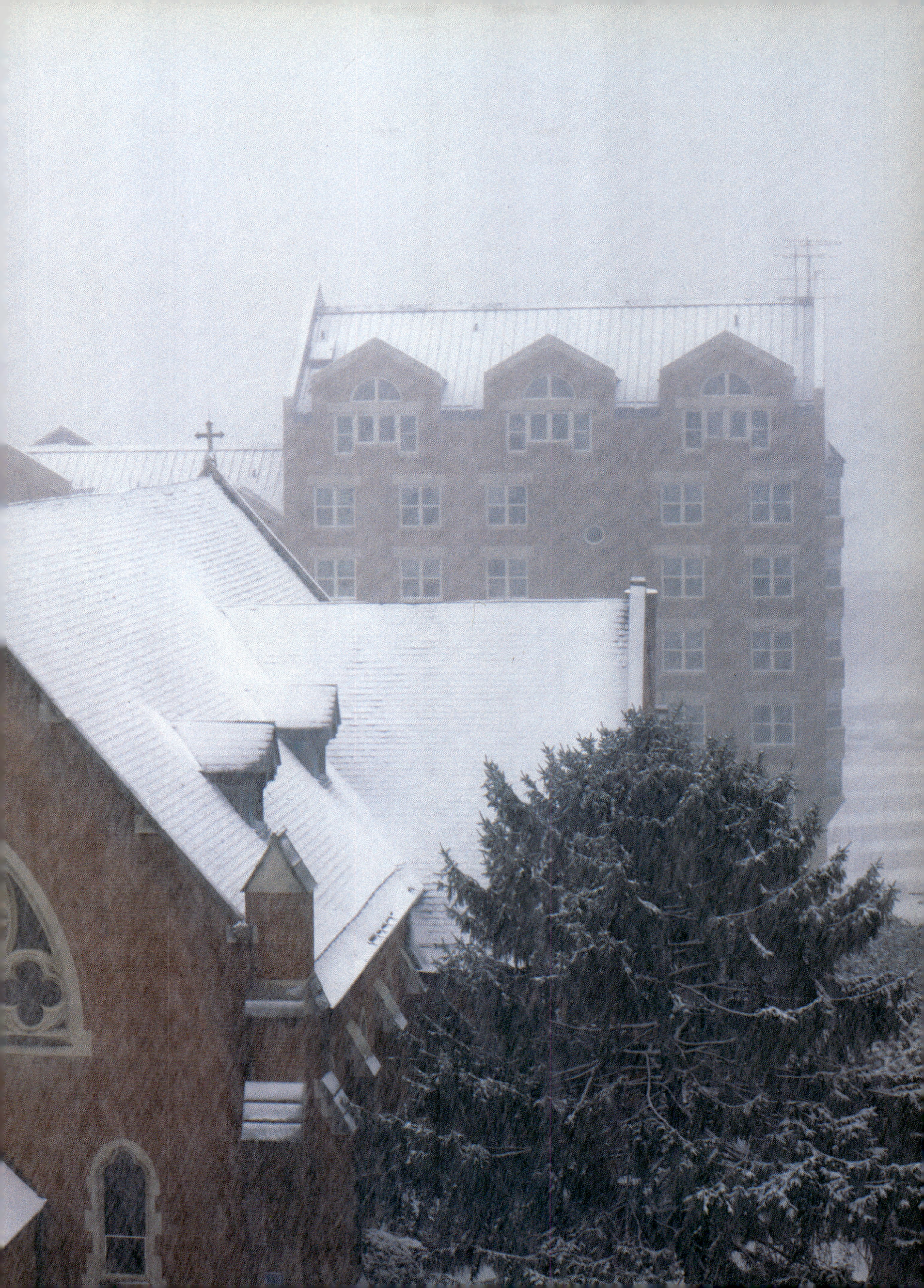

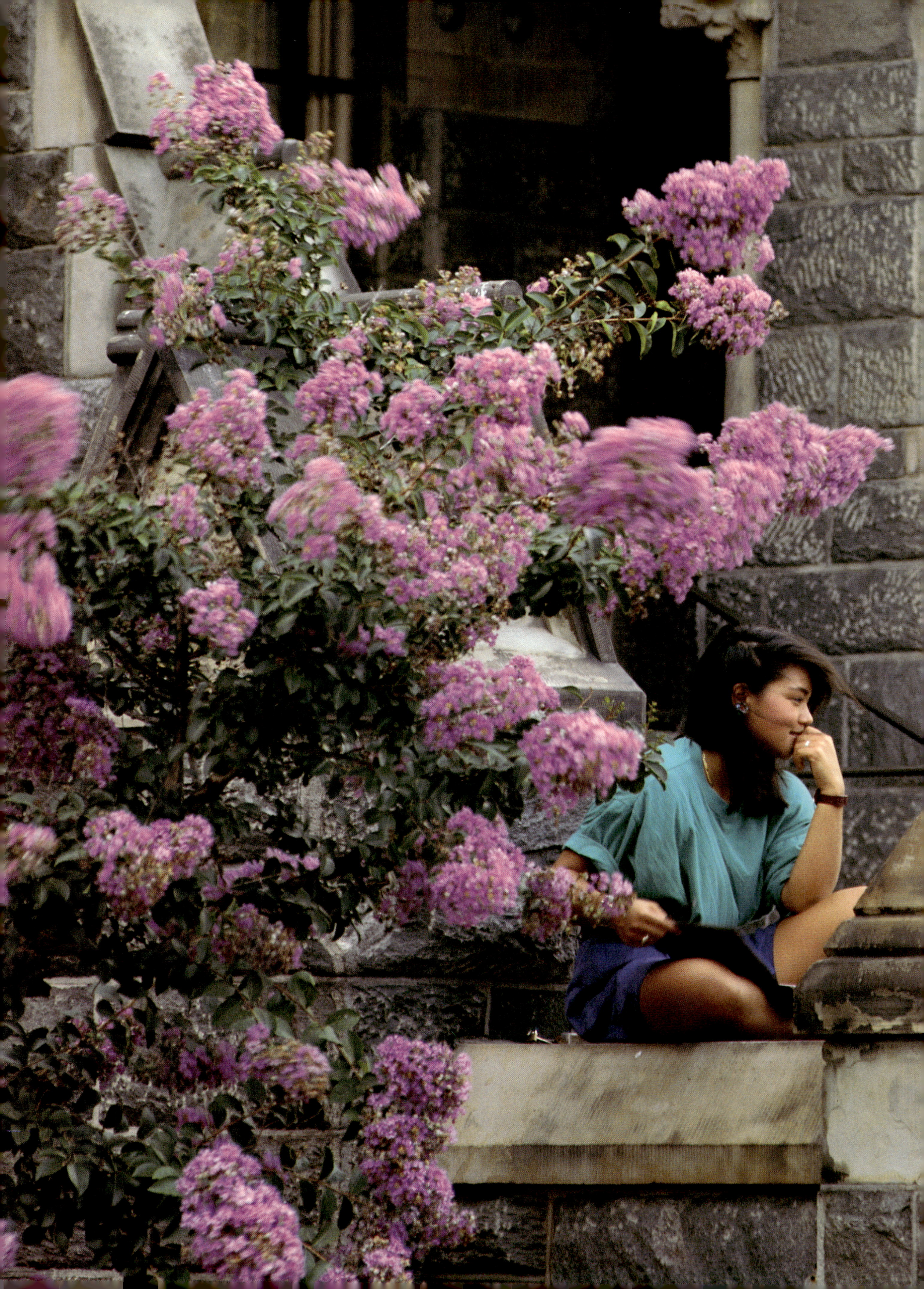

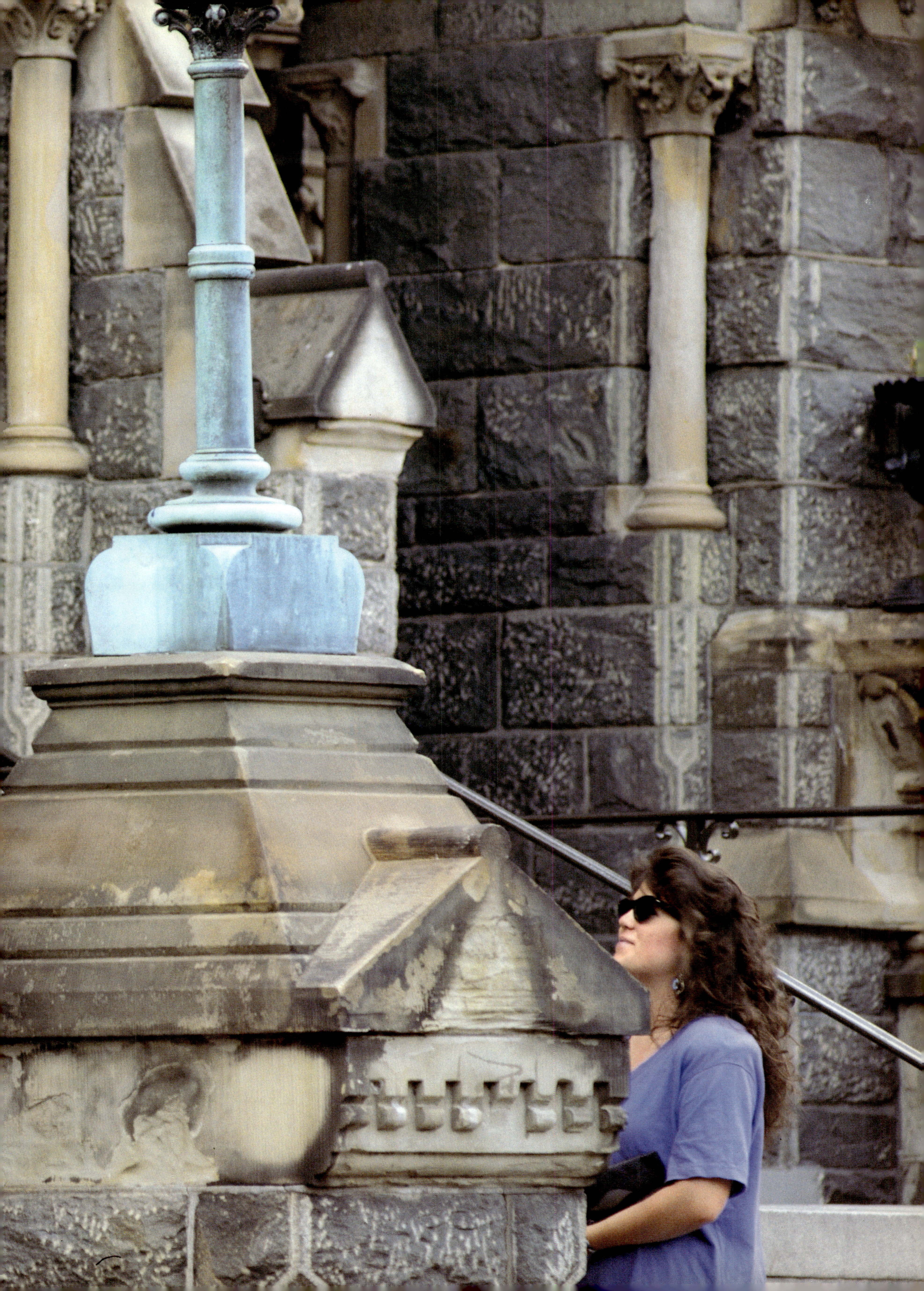

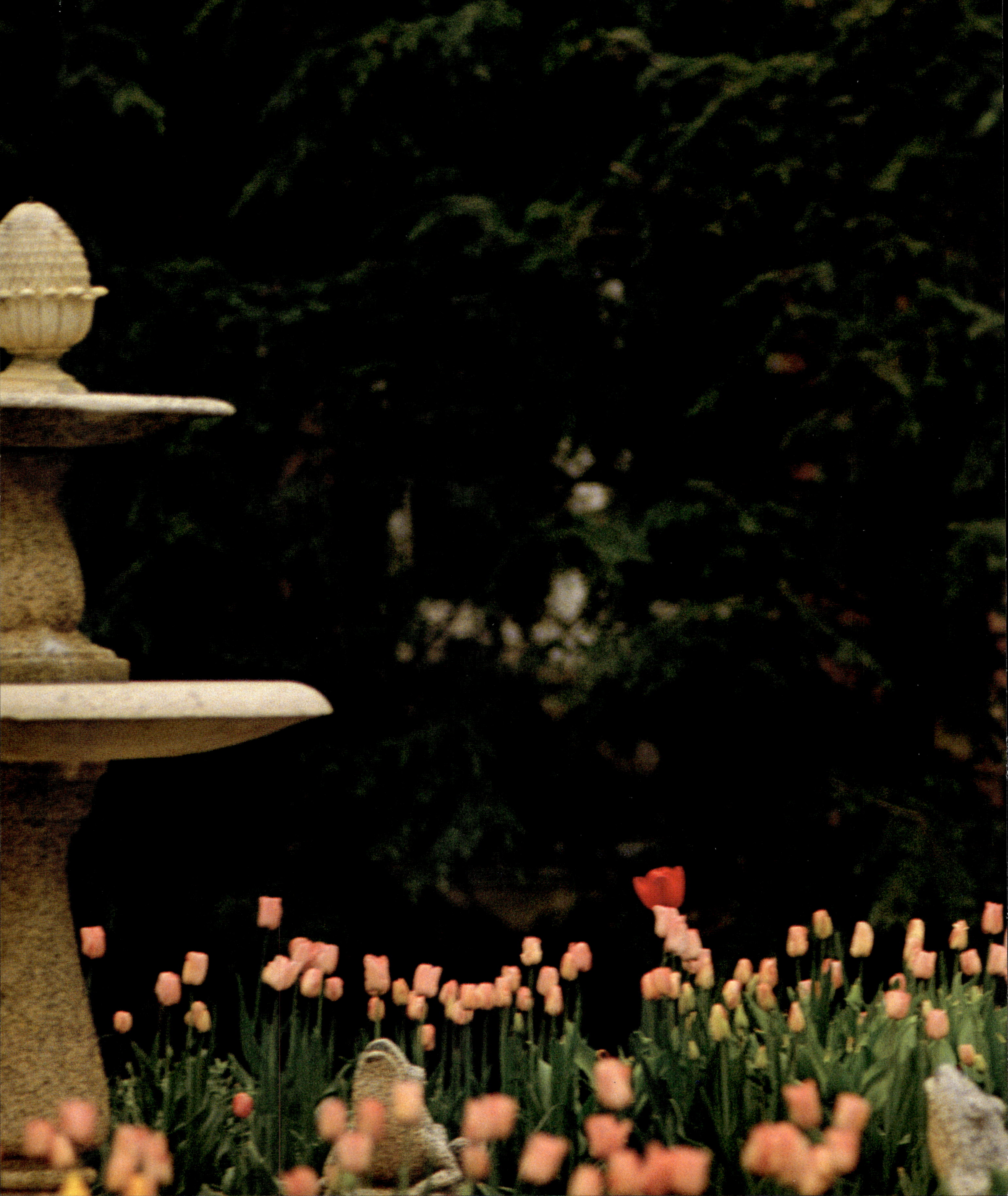

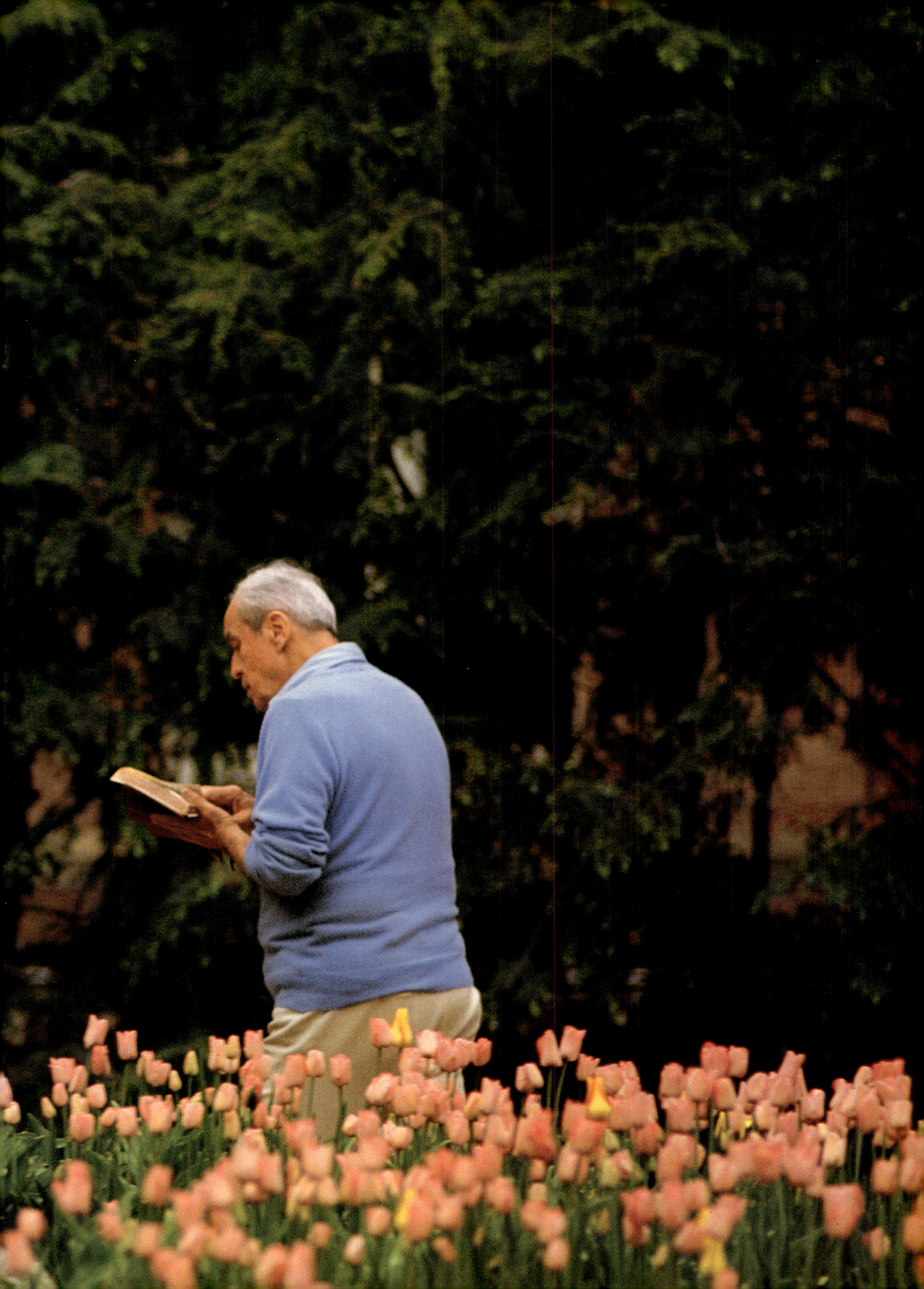

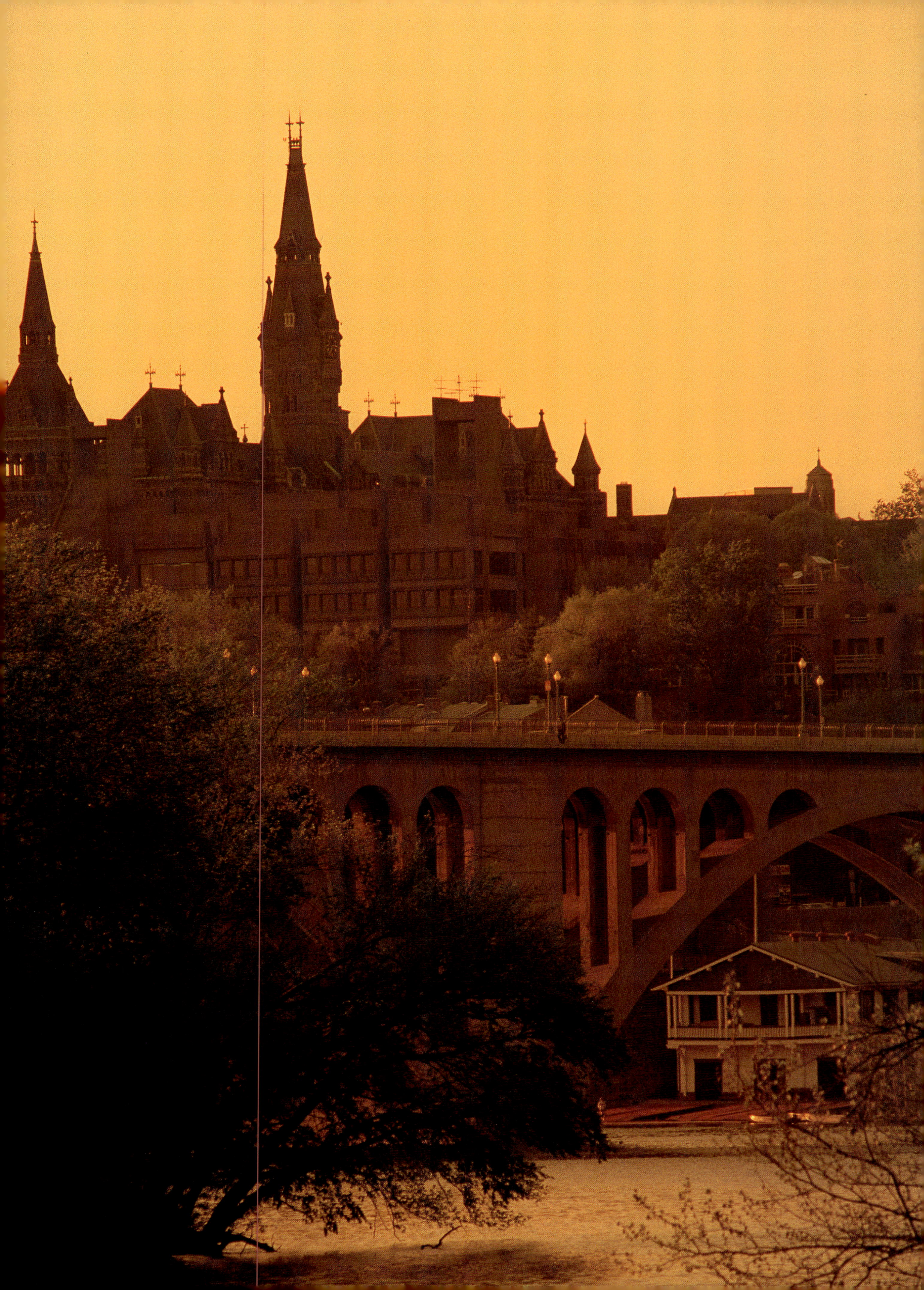

tion is rich indeed.

Georgetown by its Catholic instincts links together learning and doing in all it does, the Catholic vision that wisdom, to be complete, must lead to virtue. We know well that virtue is not taught in a lecture; it's a subtler grace than that. But we also know that all learning involves growth, and that most growth leans on models. There are many virtues no university can touch because they lie outside of the range of its works and days. But there are many that the faculty can model, and do, exquisitely. A savage probity in research, the open-heartedness of teaching, enough ironic realism to admit intellectual or moral weakness, the ingrained habit of telling the truth even to one's own cost, a tolerance of grating diversity, courage to face the discomfort of challenged assumptions, a self-giving care for others – all these virtues we do model, and well.

Just as Georgetown must cope with both river and hill, its rooted faith shapes the life of the mind with a dual vision of man and of the creation that houses him. This sacramental vision sees secular reality as more than itself, grasps the numinosity of even material fact and much more of spiritual being. Ignatius of Loyola urged on all Jesuits the vision of God as "laboring in all things under the sun," and in that he

[included]

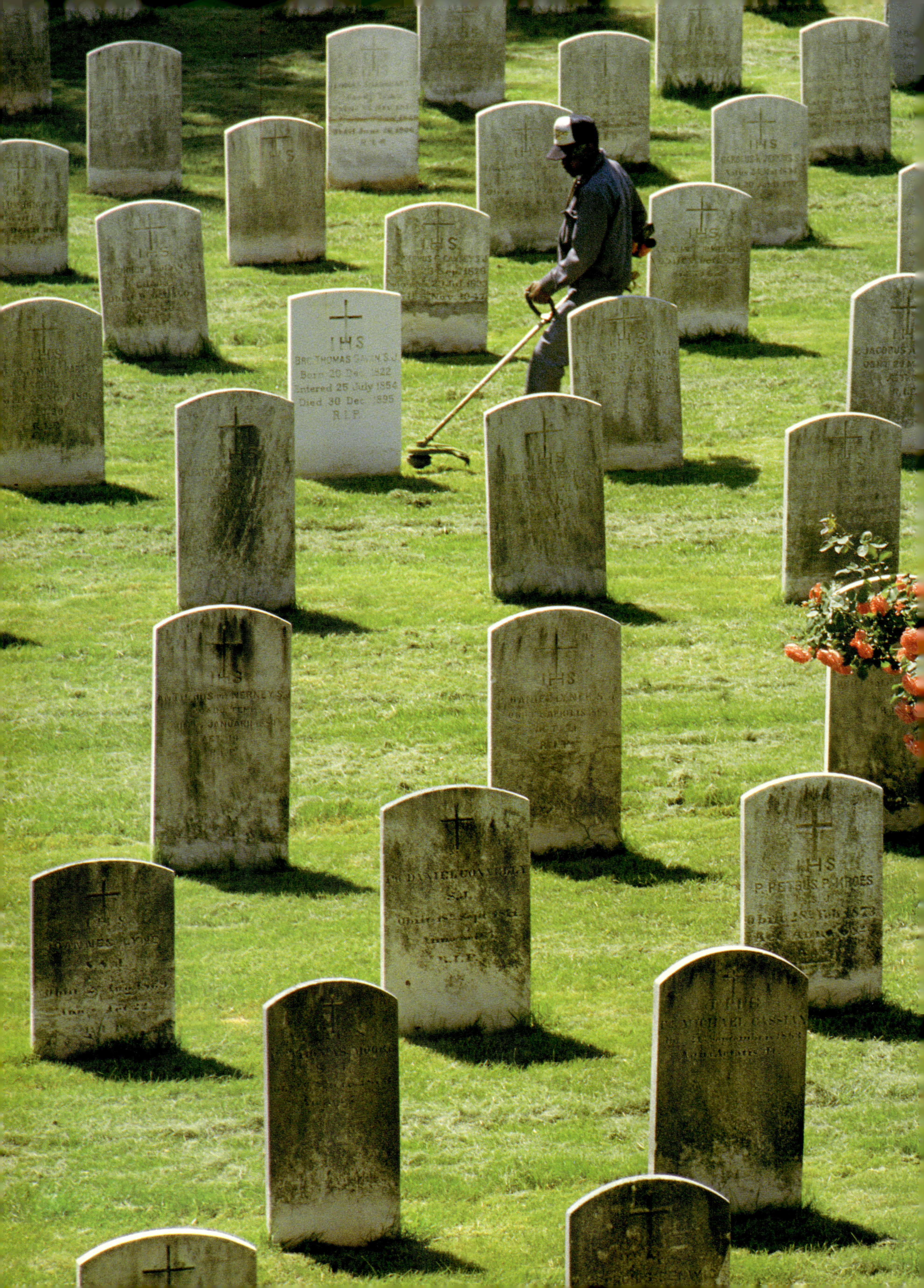
IHS
Entered 25 July 1854
Died 30 Dec 1895
R.I.P.

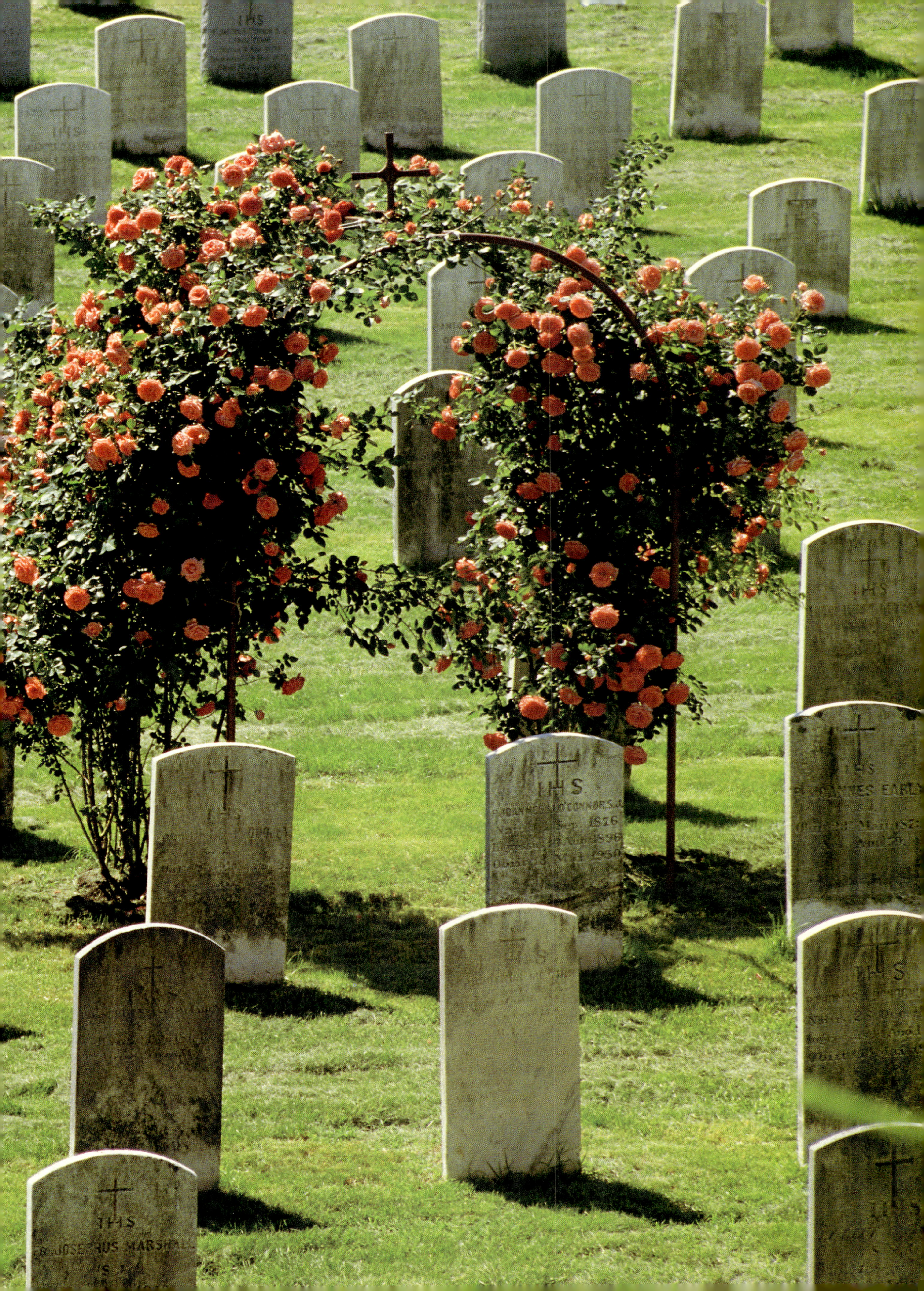
IHS
JOANNES EARLY
IHS
JOSEPHUS MARSHALL

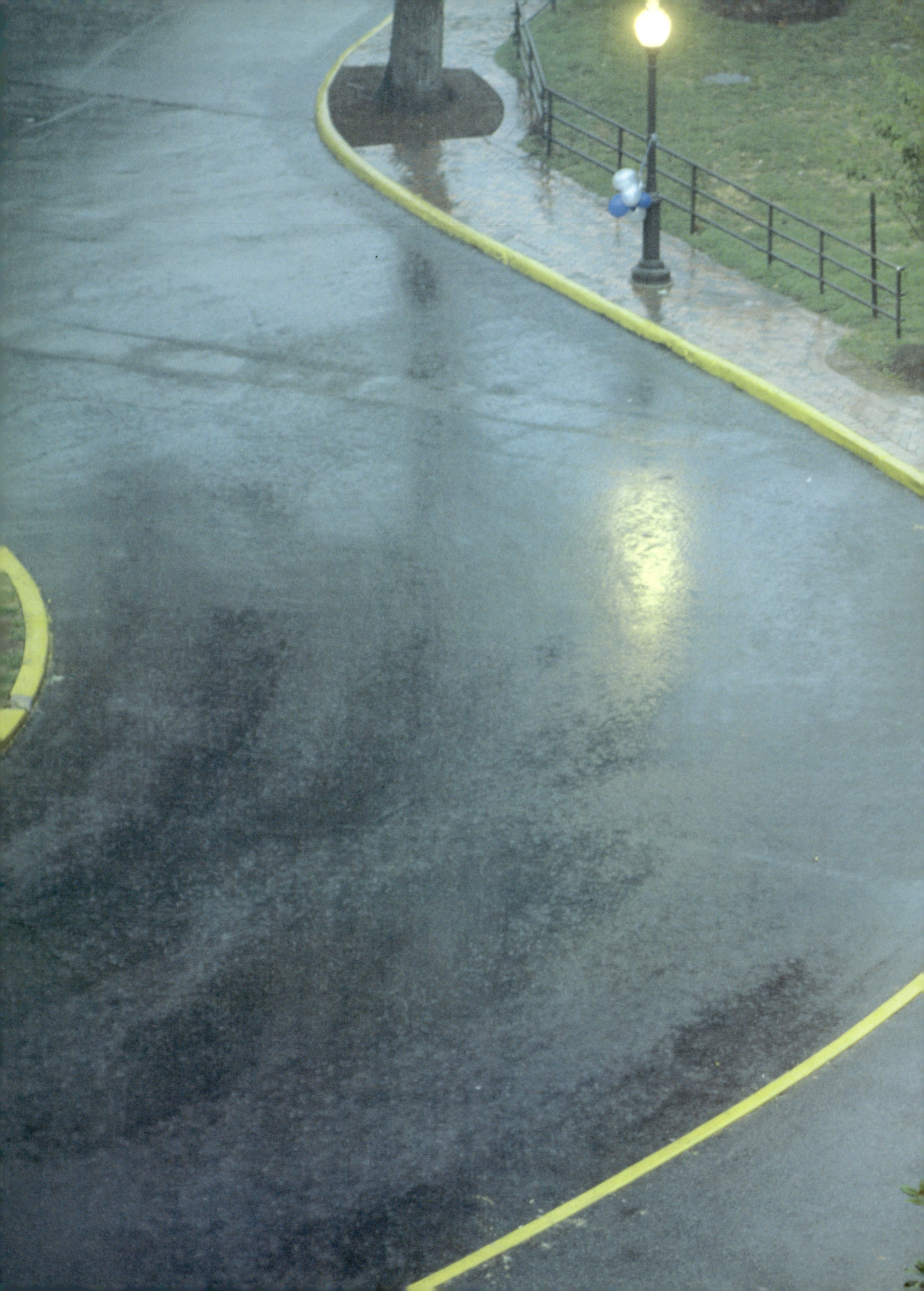

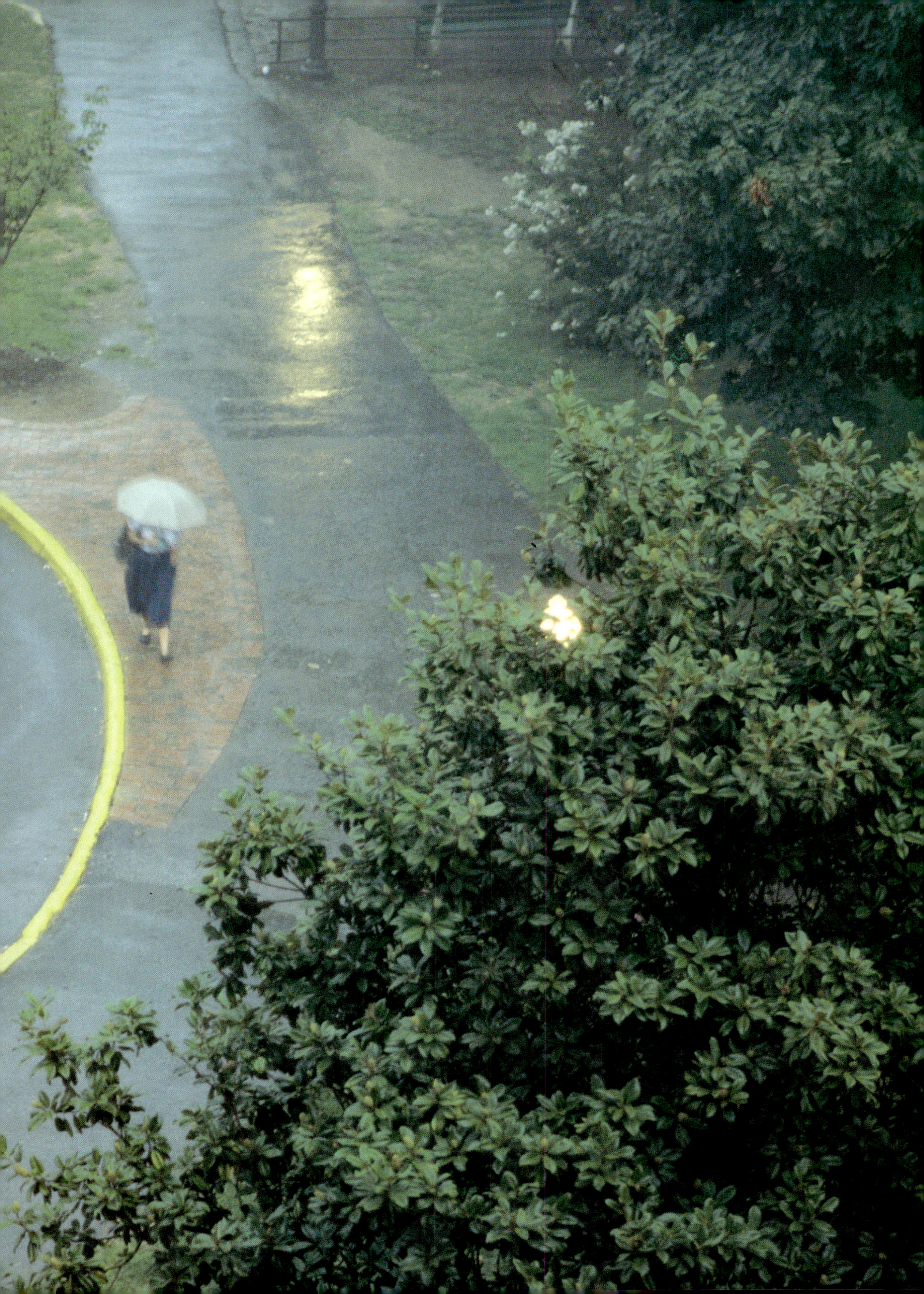

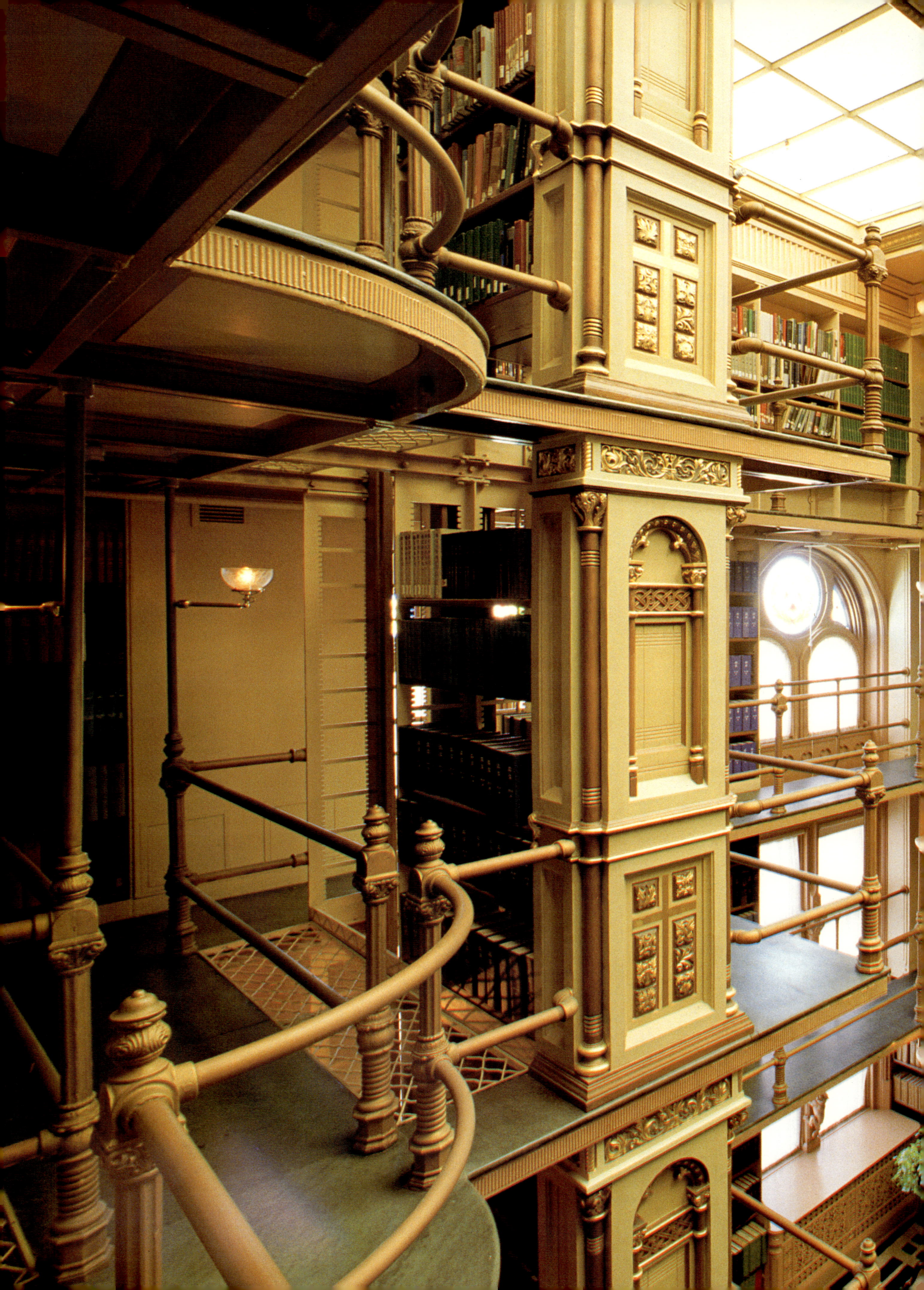

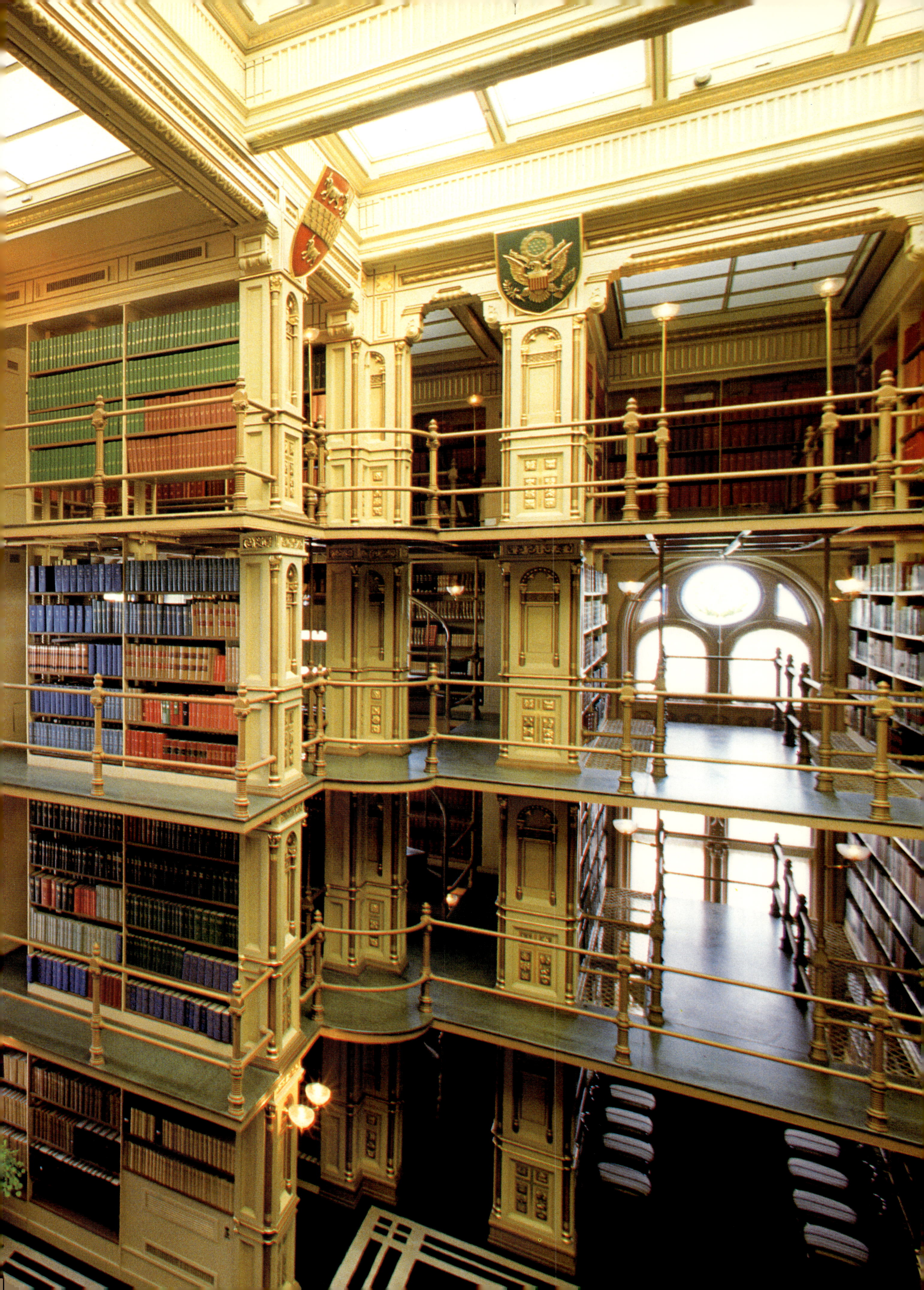

included ourselves. Of all our heritage as a Catholic institution this sacramental view is the farthest reaching. At its best it leads us beyond the contemplation that is bound by time into the contemplation that is both worship and prayer. All our striving reaches toward a world transformed – our double vision is both dream and debt.

The daily corporate act that sums up all we are and calls us into oneness far beyond anything human learning can imagine is the Mass. Here in the thronged forum of our faith is the great gathering of believers. We come to it old and young, rich and poor, learned and neophyte. We come to it in a simplicity that suits us as creatures, but knowing that in it hides the sure and certain grasp of the Creator himself.

Out of our works and days as a Catholic university came one great virtue that we proclaim simply by being what we are – the virtue of hope. That hope is human and divine, focused on the person of Jesus of Nazareth, God made man. With the echo of his footsteps still on our earth, we cannot imagine the universe abandoned by its Creator or a human mind untouched or unconditioned by his standing amongst us. That conditioning promises us that God has a purpose for his creation and for us in it, that the forces of darkness, whatever damage they do, will

[not]

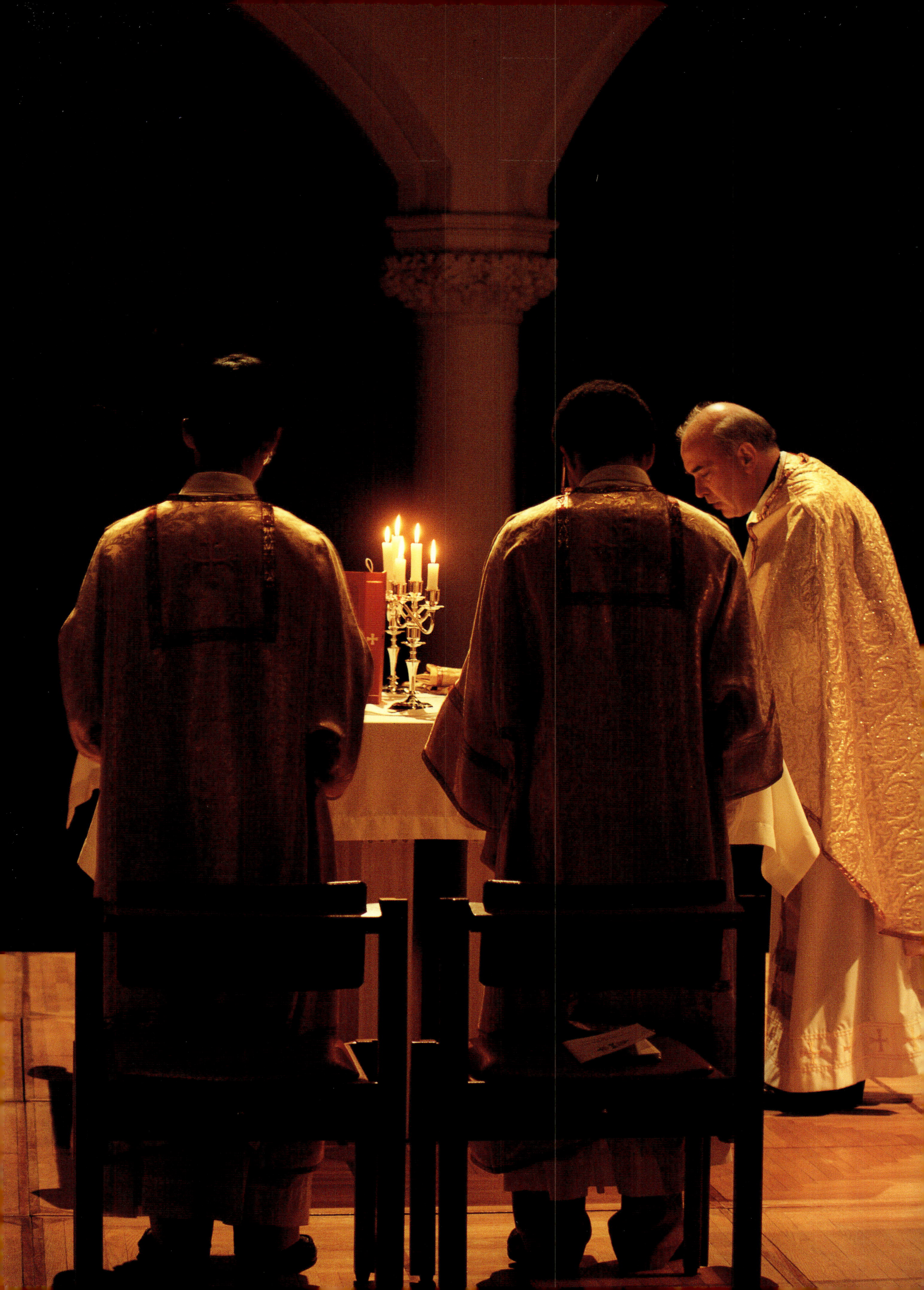

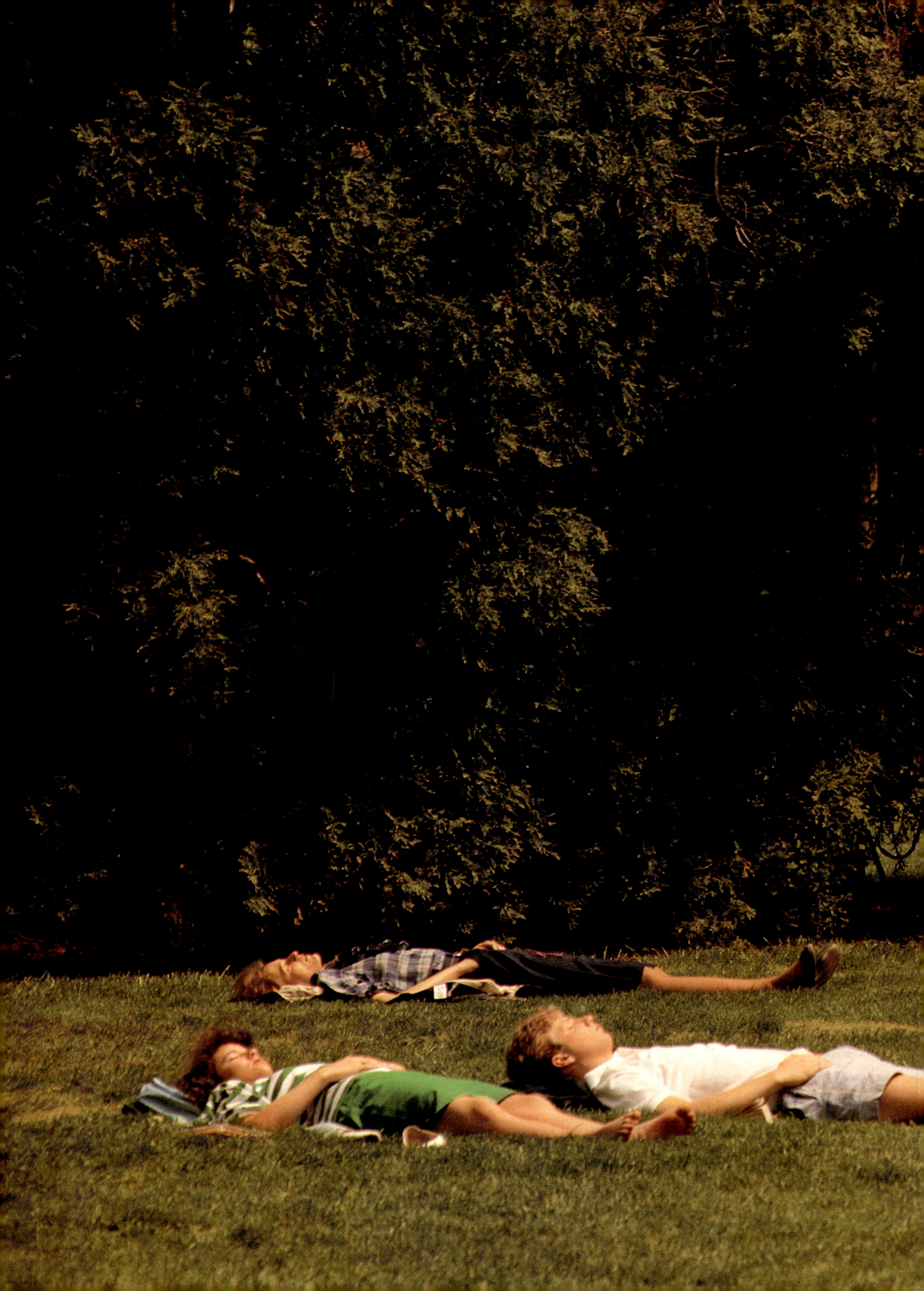

OUR LADY OF FATIMA

PAX

CLASS OF 1959

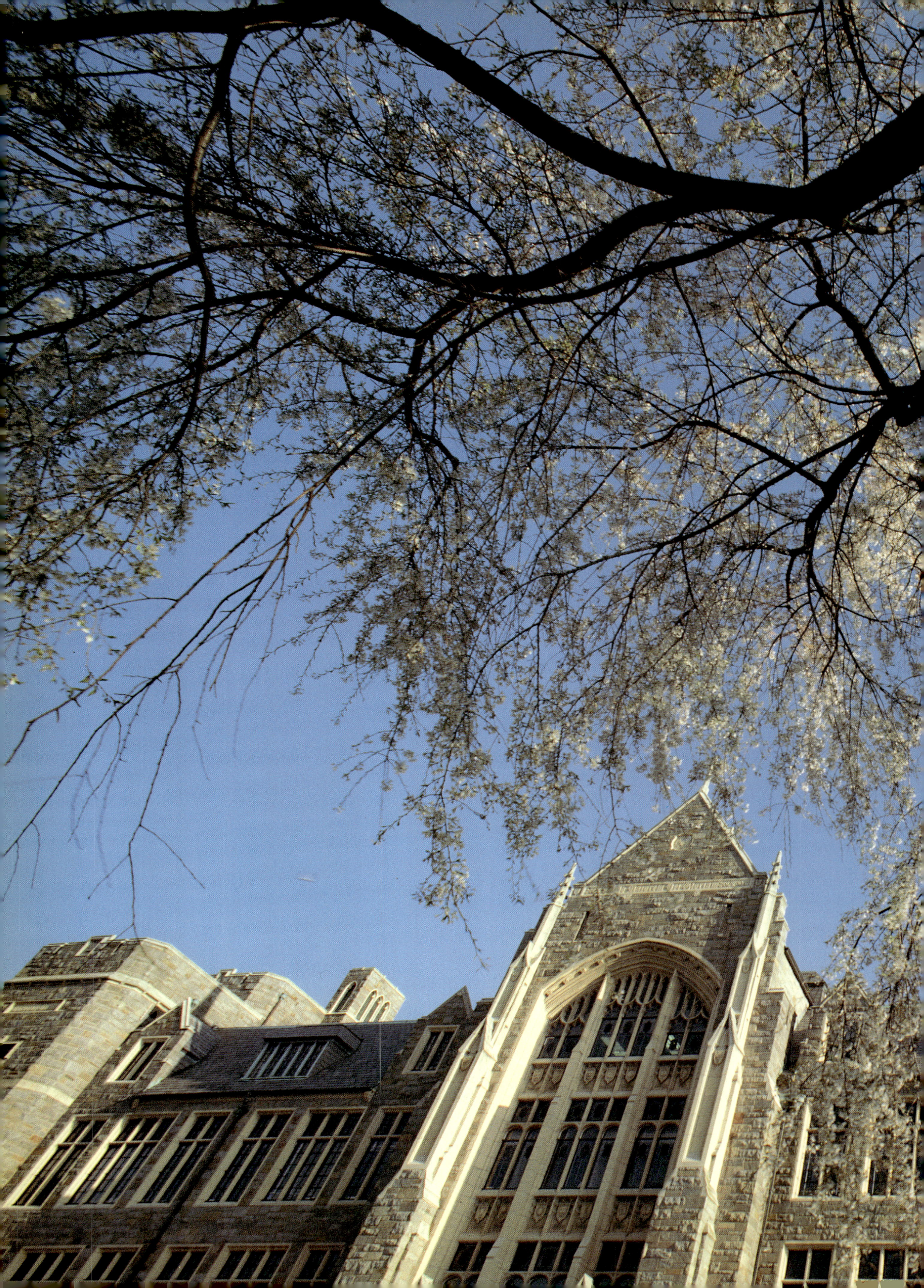

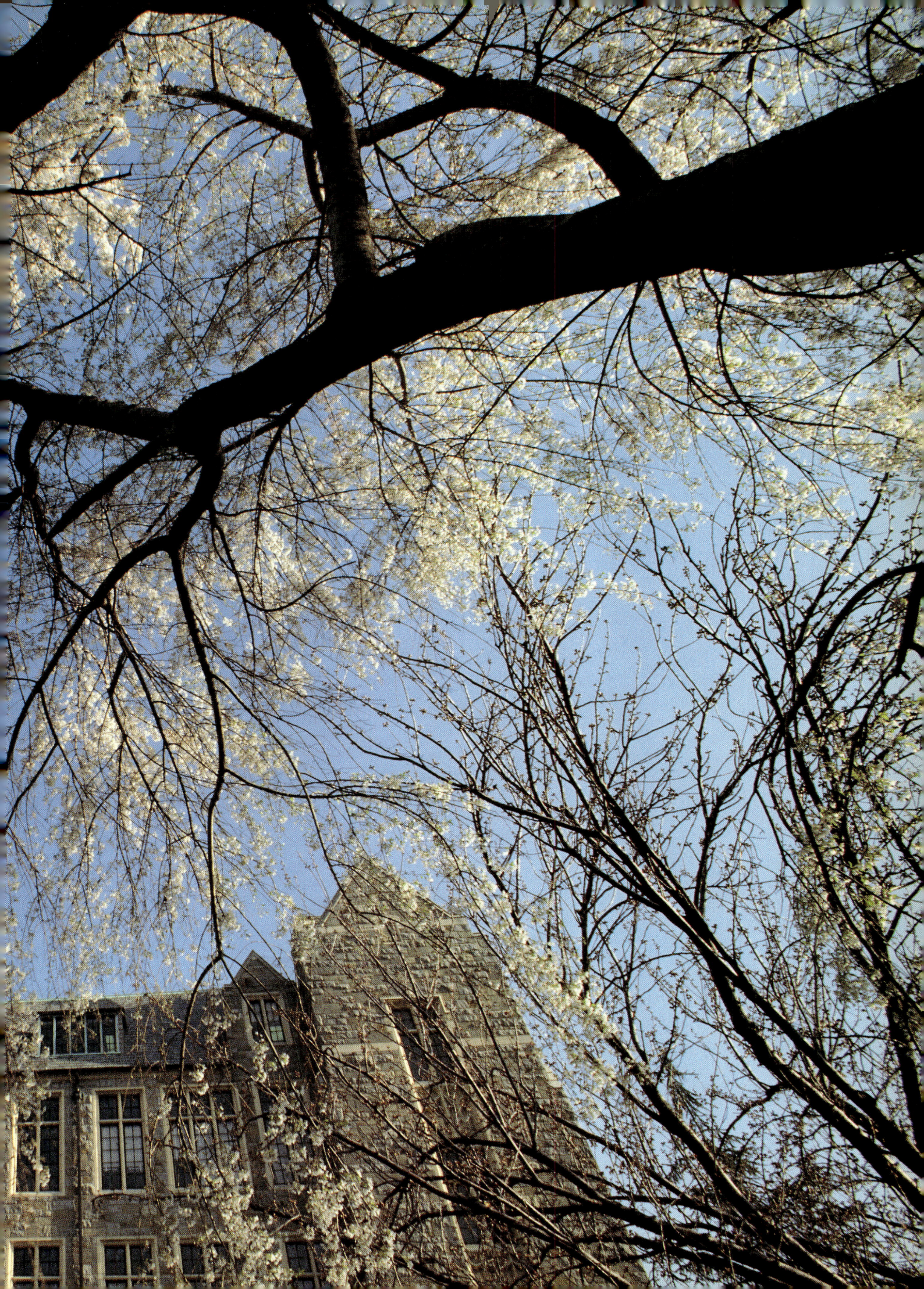

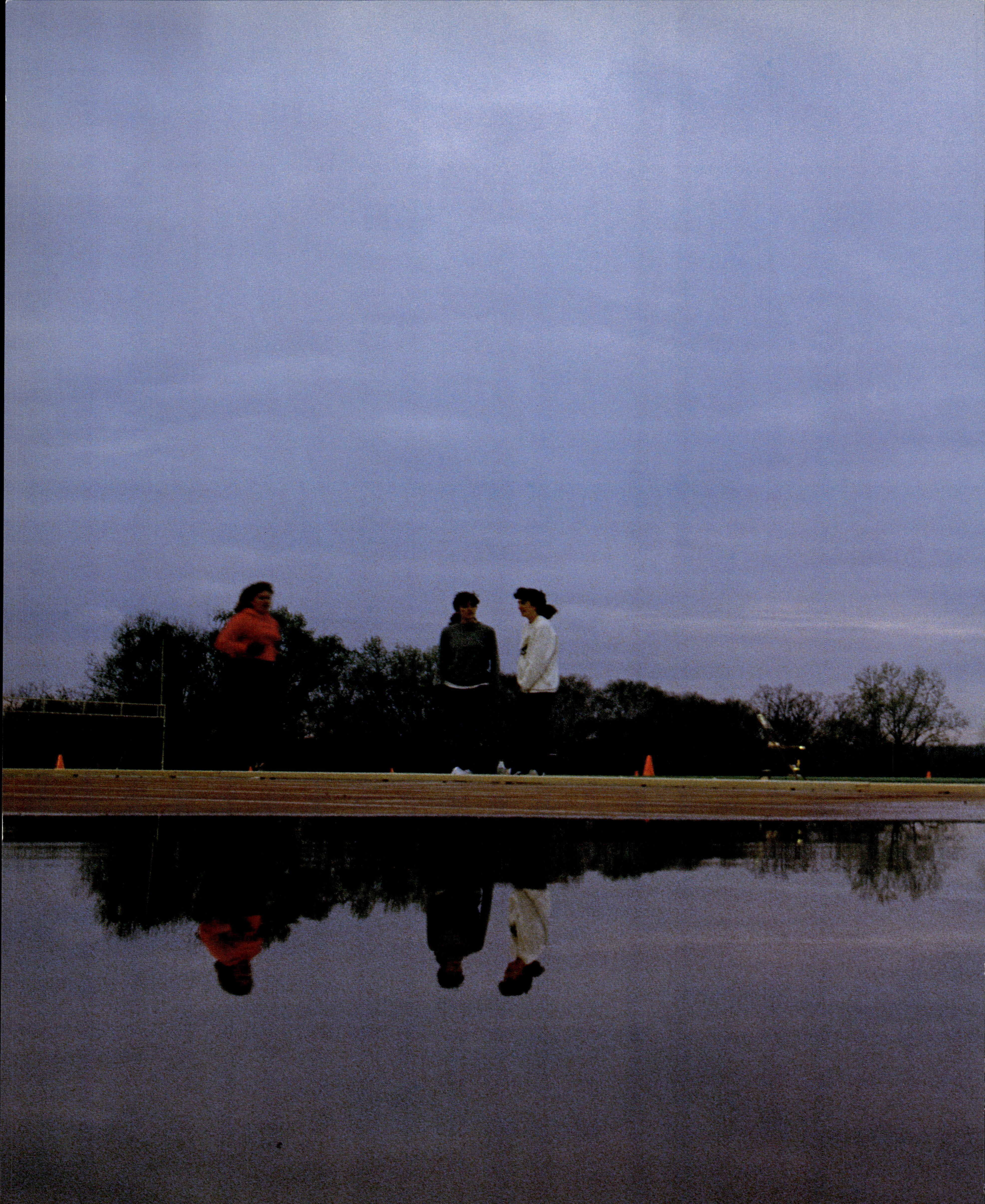

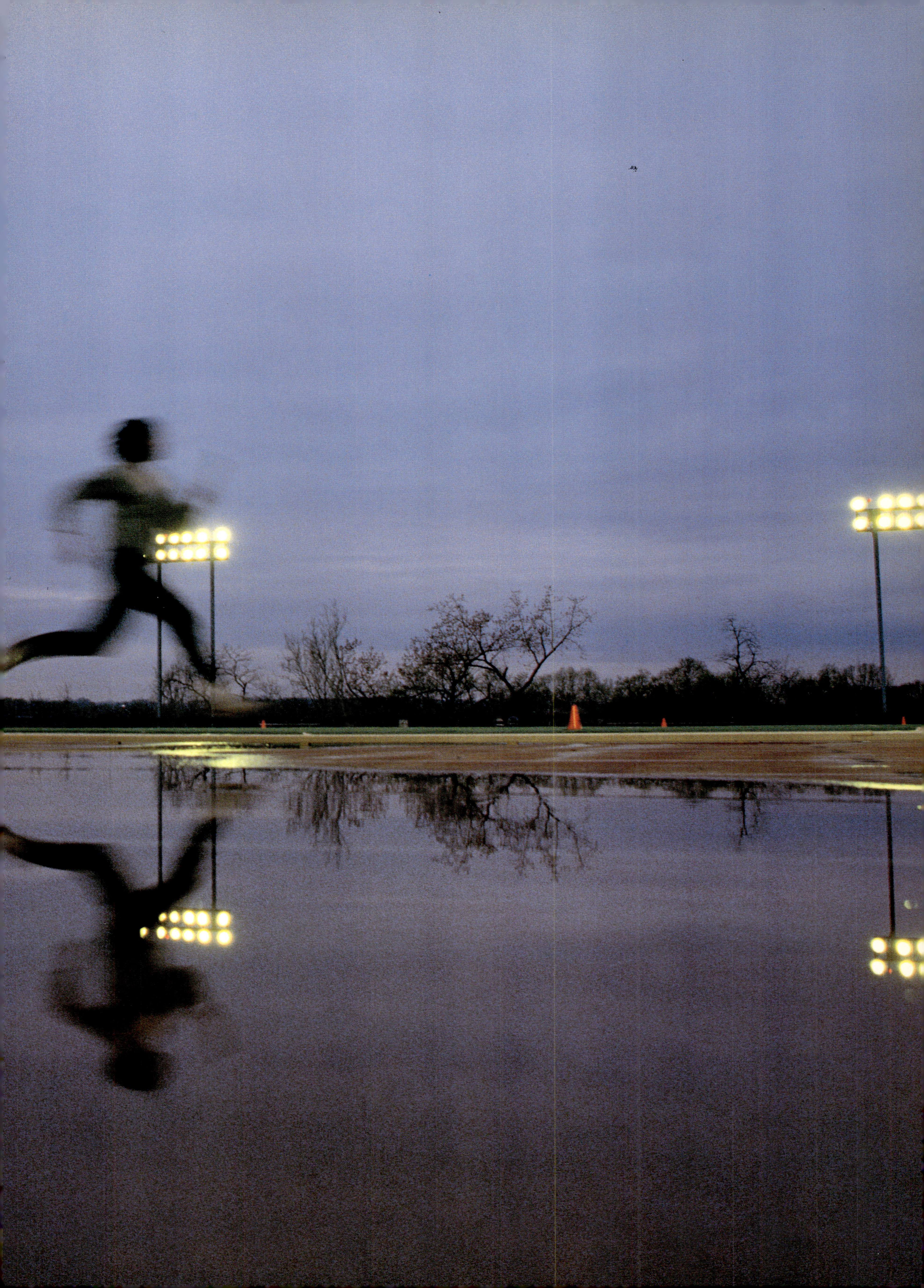

not ultimately prevail. For Catholics, everything we study, everything we learn, the best of our knowledge and the sum of our wisdom is only the "piece-bright paling" that "shuts Christ home."

In that hope, Georgetown faces its third century. All of us would be greater fools than those who came before us if we did not know that the next hundred years will be as shaken by our failures, as hurt by our weaknesses, as cramped by our fearfulness as have been the last two hundred. History will leave us staggered and sad at missed opportunities, at risks and roads not taken. But celebration is no excuse to patronize the past. To each of us is spoken the warning, "thou knowest this man's fall; thou knowest not his wrastling." Our own falls have yet to reach the tolerant gaze of chroniclers.

Humbled by that knowledge, but with prideful hope in those who come after us, we bid welcome to the years from 1989 to 2089. On this hill, by this river, amid this city, may Georgetown's heart's truth still be sung in a century's turning.

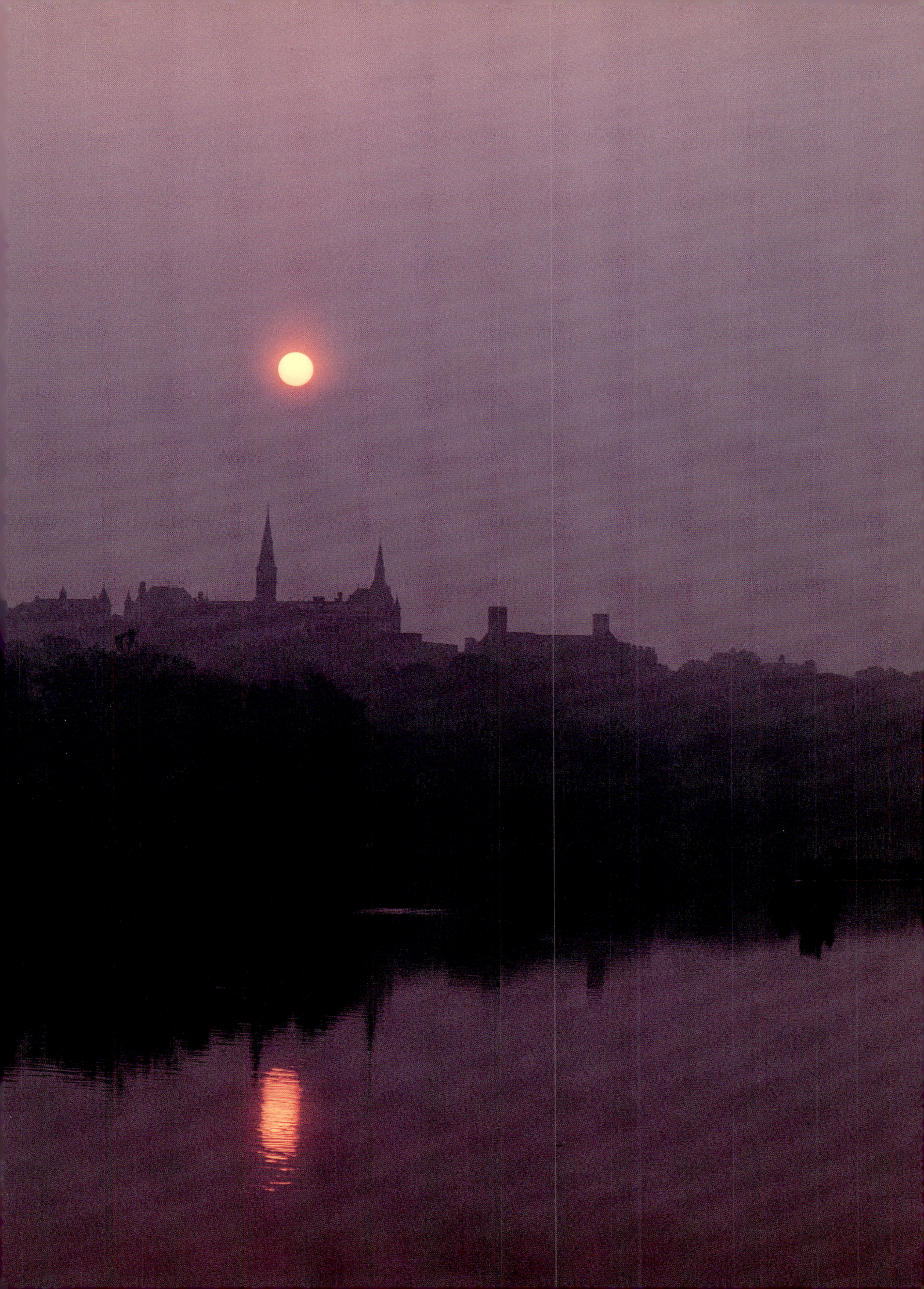

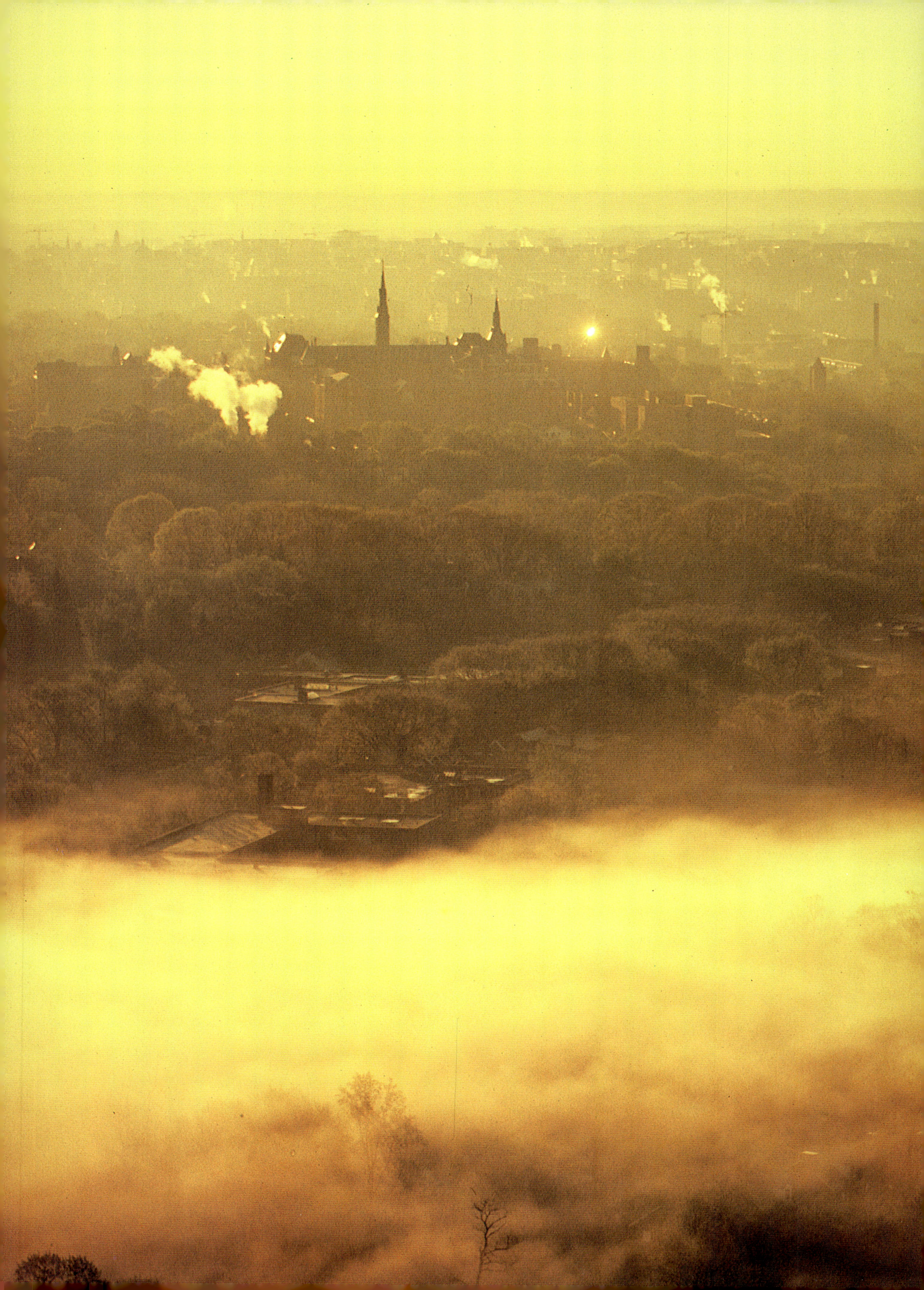

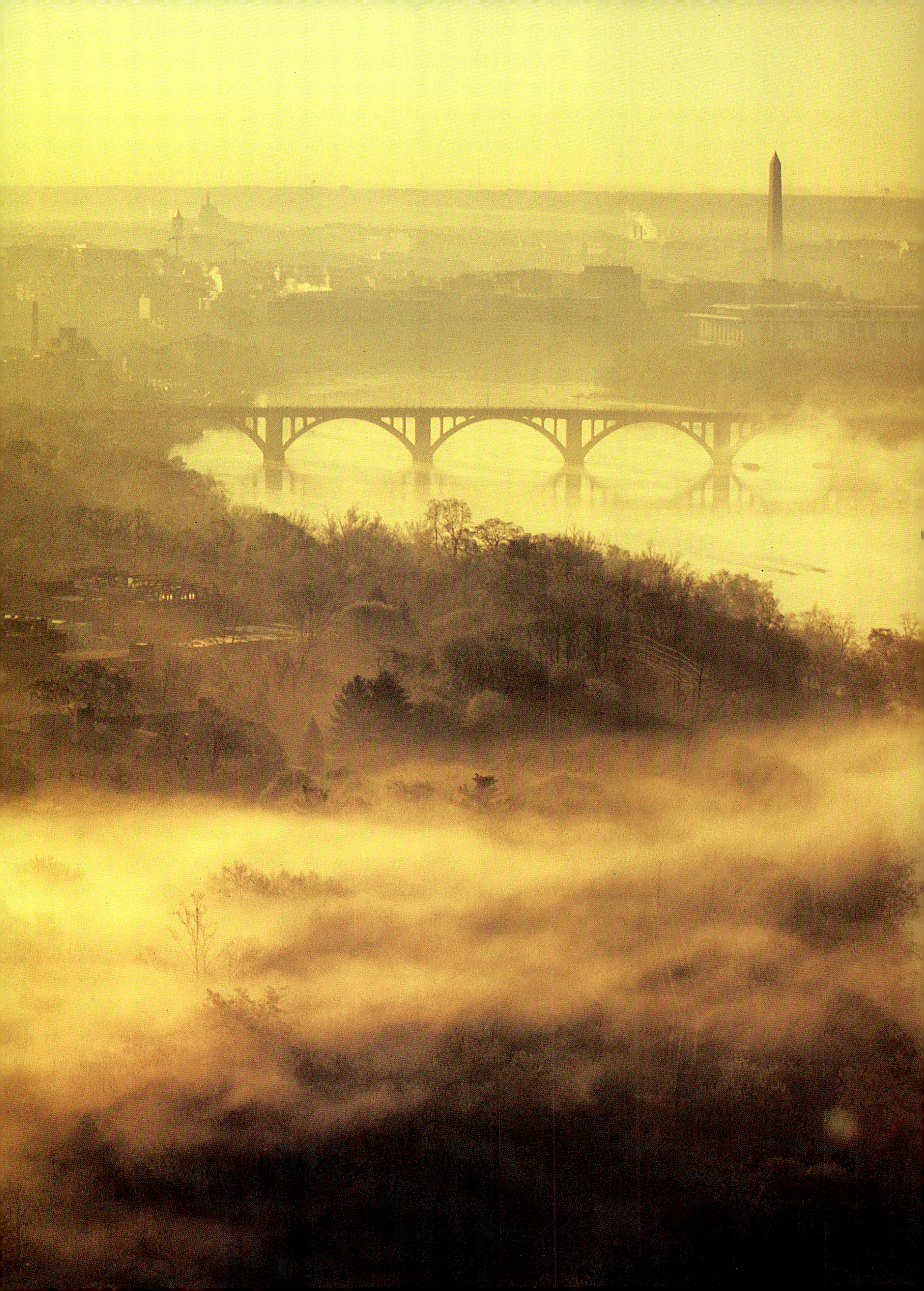

BANNERS AND PENNANTS were visible symbols of the opening of Georgetown's year-long Bicentennial celebration on October 1, 1988. At the academic convocation on Healy Lawn that day, spectators watched President Ronald Reagan receive an honorary degree against a backdrop of waving banners hung from Healy Hall's imposing Potomac bluestone granite facade.

THE POTOMAC RIVER on the south, the Medical Center complex on the north, Glover-Archbold Park on the west, and a stone wall on the east have protected Georgetown from Washington's phenomenal growth in recent years and kept it an island of learning in a sea of frenetic activity.

HEALY HALL'S CENTRAL CLOCK tower soars some 200 feet into the air, its delicate Flemish Romanesque lines belying the immensity of the building, which is made up of some 3,000 cubic feet of stone, 2,000,000 bricks and 350,000 feet of yellow Georgia pine. When it was completed in 1879, Healy Hall joined the Capitol Building as one of Washington's architectural landmarks.

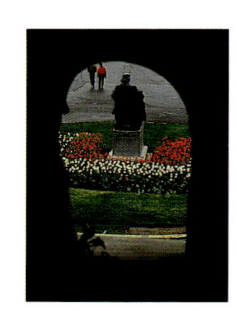

"WE SHALL BEGIN THE BUILDING of our academy this summer. In the beginning we shall confine our plan to a house of 63 or 64 ft. by 50, on one of the most lovely situations that imagination can frame. It will be three stories high, exclusive of the offices under the whole. Do not forget to give and procure assistance. On this academy is built all my hope of permanency and success to our H. Religion in the United States."
JOHN CARROLL *to Charles Plowden,*
March 1, 1788

"GEORGETOWN'S HILL is a rather minor bump along the Potomac, nowhere near as high as the neighbor hill on which the National Cathedral sits. Perhaps Carroll was willing to sacrifice height for nearness to the river. He also must have known in his bones that it is proper for cathedrals to dominate skylines, but not for universities."

THE INTERCULTURAL CENTER courtyard has become a popular gathering place for students. In the background the University's observatory sits on a green hilltop, much the way it did when it was built in 1841. The wood frame structure has not been used for astronomical observation in recent years and has been adopted by the biology department as a research site.

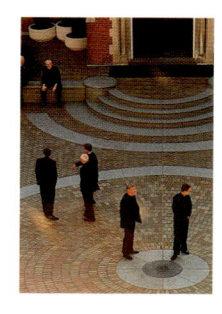

"JOHN CARROLL WOULD HAVE been quite at home with us today, in Dahlgren Chapel, in the easy talk among students and faculty, in the prayer and lives of his brother Jesuits, in the long flow of God's grace across this good ground." The courtyard shown here was recently renovated and rededicated in 1988 to the memory of the Reverend Brian McGrath, S.J.

HERE AT GEORGETOWN the Potomac turns wide and deep, rising and falling to the rhythm of the Chesapeake tides. Eighteenth-century vessels had a view much more pastoral than this one. Although the tiny port of Georgetown was bustling, the city of Washington was only a dream, and even in 1790 when it was named the capital city it was little more than some cleared fields and scattered buildings.

*Give way, give way, no man shall say
We're laggards at the oar;
No dame shall flush, nor maiden blush
For Georgetown's honest fame.
Hurrah! then, boys, hurrah! hurrah!
The Blue and Gray forever.*

*We give to thee Potomac fair,
Thou river all our own,
As trim a bark, as blithe a crew
As e'er thy waves have known.*

Boat song, COLLEGE JOURNAL, 1876

"WITH SUCH ADVANTAGES as we possess, with a beautiful river rippling right under our noses (excuse me for the unpoetical expression, but it conveys the idea) we certainly *ought* to possess a Boat Club."

from the COLLEGE JOURNAL, 1876

HEALY HALL was constructed in 1879, nearly a century after Georgetown's founding. A prime example of its architectural eclecticism is the brick facade opposite the Dahlgren Chapel. Though well known for its stone-constructed front, Healy Hall displays a rear side that is a nineteenth-century Victorian interpretation of the Federal style of Old North. This facade, finished in brick, connects Old North and Maguire to frame the courtyard.

THE STEPS TO THE ESPLANADE in front of White-Gravenor Hall have become a transition from the old Georgetown to the new. They connect the Depression-era stone structure to the brick courtyard of the Intercultural Center, a new addition to the campus in 1982 and now a center of undergraduate academic activity.

THIS JUXTAPOSITION of the Healy Building and the Washington Monument is a reminder of the strong relationship between the University and the city, one that John Carroll anticipated but could never have fully imagined. As the Healy construction was being completed in 1879, work on the Washington Monument, having been stalled for years over design arguments, was just resuming.

ONE OF THE MOST STRIKING features of the new Thomas and Dorothy Leavey Center, which opened in 1988, is its long hallway. The south wall, all glass, offers new perspectives on Healy Hall and the older part of the campus from the comfortable lounge sections that run its length.

THE GEORGETOWN "YARD" has existed in some form since Old North was completed a few years after the establishment of John Carroll's new academy. For nearly a century students walked the open space between Old South and Old North. In 1879 the Healy Building joined those two buildings, closing in the east end of the yard. In 1892 Dahlgren Chapel did the same on the west, creating the courtyard as we know it today. As a Bicentennial project, the courtyard underwent major renovation in 1988.

THE CORNER WHERE the Healy Building and Old North meet is a study in Georgetown eclecticism, with architectural styles spanning three centuries. Old North is classic eighteenth-century Federal style, the brick back of the Healy Building shows strong nineteenth-century Victorian influences, while the roofline is pure seventeenth century.

THESE STEPS DESCEND from the Intercultural Center's Galleria to its auditorium. The building opened in 1982, and while its name captures Georgetown's international heritage, its physical appearance looks forward to the next century with a dramatic expanse of photovoltaic cells on its sloped roof to capture energy from the sun. The inscription above these stairs is from the Jesuit philosopher Pierre Teilhard de Chardin, S.J.: "The age of nations is past. It remains for us now, if we do not wish to perish, to set aside the ancient prejudices and build the earth."

GEORGETOWN PLAYED its first baseball game in 1870, losing to Columbian College 23-17. In an attempt to redress the insult, they lost a second time 30-16 in a game that mercifully was called because of darkness at the end of the sixth inning. A few years later the *College Journal* described the team with this report: "Our best pitcher did not discover, until informed by others, that he curved his balls." By the end of the century Georgetown was playing Harvard, Yale, Princeton, Cornell, Navy and other leading collegiate powers. During that last decade of the century the team won three-fourths of its games.

"I REMEMBER THE SOUND of Healy's bells striking every quarter hour day and night, in sunshine and in rain through the years in College and Medical School; a vibrant fiber binding school to student, student to student, student to school; ringing for all alike – teacher, pupil, visitor, official – demanding, teaching, pleasant, insistent. Time to study, time to play, time to teach, time to pray, time . . . Time . . . Time . . . evanescent, inexorable, gossamer . . . reality."
EDWIN W. PASSARELLI, BSM. '30, MD '32

GASTON HALL is one of the Healy Building's many hidden treasures. It was not completed until 1901, some twenty years after the building opened. Its interior decorations were the work of Brother Francis Schroen. The shields above the allegorical figures recall the continental schools to which persecuted English and American Catholics sent their children.

"THE OBJECT of the proposed institution is, to unite the Means of communicating Science with an effectual Provision for guarding and improving the Morals of Youth. . . . The Benefit of this Establishment should be as general as the Attainment of its Object is desirable. It will, therefore, receive Pupils as soon as they have learned the first Elements of Letters, and will conduct them, through the several Branches of classical Learning, to that Stage of Education, from which they may proceed, with Advantage, to the study of the higher Sciences . . ."
JOHN CARROLL, *Proposals for Establishing an Academy*, 1787

COMMENCEMENT 1988 TOOK place on a stage erected in front of the Healy Building, just as it has for more than a century. The following account from the *New York Herald* of June 27, 1878, describes the same scene in front of a Healy Hall just nearing completion: "A steady stream of carriages and two lines of horse cars, laden with gayly dressed people, toiled the ascent of Georgetown heights this morning, braving the heat of the broiling sun in their desire to attend the closing exercises of the year at Georgetown College. . . . Pending the opening of the exercises the audience took advantage of the interval to inspect the new building which is to supplant the old college and is already well advanced. Its beautiful proportions delineated in the architect's plans are clearly indicated in the massive towers and stories of blue gneiss rock which are rising out of the ground and closing in one side of the quadrangle. . . . In fact, the imposing splendor of the new college will make it unrecognizable to all old graduates who come to visit the alma mater of their youth."

IN THE JESUIT AND LIBERAL arts tradition, education is the juxtaposition and intermingling of all the academic disciplines, and at times in Georgetown's two centuries space limitations have contributed to philosophic goals in unintended ways. This science laboratory is in White-Gravenor Hall, and is perhaps one of the few in the country to include among its facilities leaded windows and stained glass.

"DEMOCRATIC NATIONS CARE but little for what has been, but they are haunted by visions of what will be; in this direction their unbounded imagination grows and dilates beyond all measure.... Democracy, which shuts the past against the poet, opens the future before him."
ALEXIS DE TOCQUEVILLE
Democracy in America

ALTHOUGH HEALY HALL'S graceful and imposing central clock tower dominates the building's exterior, this view is memorable for anyone who has walked its halls. Empty or crowded, dark or filled with afternoon light spilling in from the courtyard, Healy's first floor hallway is a part of every student's life.

THE HEALY BUILDING has undergone many metamorphoses in the century since it was built. Library, laboratory, classrooms and dormitory have expanded to other buildings as the University has grown, and offices have taken over much of Healy Hall. But the Carroll Parlor (shown here) just inside the front door – a rich collection of paintings, furniture and other memorabilia – is a gentle reminder of another time and a Georgetown today's students never knew.

Howl, howl, howl, howl! O, You are men of stones,
Had I your tongues and eyes, I'd use them so
That heaven's vault should crack.
WILLIAM SHAKESPEARE
King Lear

Cry 'Havoc!' and let slip the dogs of war.
WILLIAM SHAKESPEARE
Julius Caesar

Hickey, Hickey, hai-kai!
Muckey, muckey, hay-I!
Georgetown! Georgetown! Georgetown!
College Cheer, c. 1905

THE REVEREND Joseph T. Durkin, S.J., is, among other things Georgetown's resident historian, including among his books two on the University's history. Though more than halfway through his eighth decade (nearly half of them at Georgetown) at the time of the University's two hundredth anniversary, Father Durkin, a professor emeritus of history, directed the research of a group of students in a special Bicentennial class he taught on Georgetown history.

"THE ANTITHESIS BETWEEN a technical and a liberal education is fallacious. There can be no adequate technical education which is not liberal, and no liberal education which is not technical: that is, no education which does not impart both technique and intellectual vision. In simpler language, education should turn out the pupil with something he knows well and something he can do well. This intimate union of practice and theory aids both."
ALFRED NORTH WHITEHEAD
The Aims of Education

"CRAS AMET qui nunquam amavit quique amavit cras amet." In one sense the Renaissance, and for that matter the Baroque, are reborn with each freshman class.

"THE FEDERAL CUCKOO in our nest has probably given more shape to Georgetown than any other force brought to bear on it. For the hundreds of students who work on 'The Hill' or in the bureaucracy, anywhere indeed in the federal Escorial, Georgetown does not need to lift a finger to rivet them for life to the innards and habits, as well as, thank God, to the dreams of democracy." This photograph is a window view from the Edward Bennett Williams Law Library.

"APPRECIATING THE BENEFITS of the instruction accorded me, I promise to esteem and revere the teachers who have trained me in the science and art of medicine, to share my good fortune with them and to relieve their necessities should want befall them.... With purity of purpose and holiness of life, I will practice my profession.... As long as I keep this promise, I hope to enjoy happiness in life, success in my profession, the respect of my fellow men. But may the reverse be my lot if I should willfully violate my solemn word now given before God."
from the Oath of Hippocrates

GEORGETOWN'S MEDICAL school opened in 1851 at 12th and F Streets, N.W., with two lecture rooms, an anatomy laboratory, a dispensary and an infirmary accommodating six patients. In 1930 it moved to its present location on Reservoir Road, and though the building's classic federal exterior remains, the interior has undergone total renovation. This view is of the school's anatomy laboratory, still a central part of medical education.

THIS CENTRAL ATRIUM just inside the entrance foyer of the Georgetown Law Center's Edward Bennett Williams Law Library is a contemporary evocation of the rotundas of its neighboring classic federal buildings like the Capitol Building and Library of Congress. The new law library, which opened in 1989, virtually doubled the Law Center's physical space.

FOR NEARLY A CENTURY since its construction in 1892, Dahlgren Chapel has had a westward view toward the Potomac and the distant Virginia hills, but the Village C residence halls, added a few years ago, have embraced the chapel and added a new western perimeter to the old "quad" area of the campus.

"THE OLD FRIENDS of this venerable institution will soon cease to recognize it, except from the rear. A magnificent new building, more than three hundred feet long and five stories high, built in the most solid manner, of stone, now connects and completely hides, from the front, the two lines of old buildings, which, thus become merely wings. It is not yet finished, but will be ready for use by next session. The old college ought to increase its students largely and rapidly, with so magnificent an addition to its accommodations."
ACADEMY JOURNAL
Alexandria, Va., 1879

"OUR FOCUS on the act of contemplation, rather than on the objects of it, solves several problems. First, we can contemplate everything, or at least everything that touches either truth or beauty, and few of our subjects would flee from their embrace. Second we see more clearly why 'knowledge is its own end' was so strong a premise for John Henry Newman, and why he found it so important in describing a Catholic university. Finally, academic contemplation starts us on the long road that leads us beyond the root incompleteness of all created things. Beyond the contemplative works and days of any university lie the vast realms of theological contemplation, 'the intuitive gaze at God as known through reason enlightened by faith.'"
TIMOTHY S. HEALY, S.J.

THE VIEW OF THE GEORGETOWN skyline from Roosevelt Island at the bend of the Potomac has attracted artists for years, especially since the addition of the Healy Building with its imposing spires. Late afternoon light adds a final touch as the setting sun sinks low on the river and briefly lights the arches under the Key Bridge.

THE JESUIT CEMETERY was once at the edge of the campus, but it has now been surrounded on all sides by new buildings. At the very center of the University resides this quiet reminder of those who gave their lives for its betterment.

*Lead, kindly Light, amid the encircling
  gloom;
Lead thou me on!
The night is dark, and I am far from
  home;
Lead thou me on!
Keep thou my feet: I do not ask to see
The distant scene; one step enough for me.*
JOHN HENRY CARDINAL NEWMAN

THE RIGGS LIBRARY underwent major renovation in 1982. Although the Lauinger Library now serves as the main library of the University, Riggs remains a repository for part of the collection. Its chief function today, however, is as a setting for special university functions – board meetings, lectures, dinners and receptions.

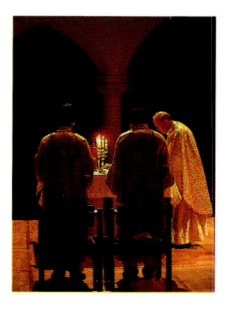

"IF THE MASS IS CATHOLICISM IN miniature, the Mass is Georgetown at its most Catholic.... Despite so much that distresses, the deep spirituality of uncounted Georgetown Catholics thrills me. Whether they recognize it or not, such profound oneness with a God they love above all else and with sisters and brothers they prize as images of God has to be grounded in the Eucharistic center of Catholic existence. It stems in large measure from a graced people that gathers each Sunday across the world in a single glorious act of community worship."
WALTER J. BURGHARDT, S.J.

THE COLLEGE EXPERIENCE is one of contrasts, both real and figurative, though sometimes the two appear at the same time.

"WITH EDUCATION and scientific research on the march, Georgetown today can ill afford to continue along the even tenor of her way. She must forge ahead if she is to add new luster to her escutcheon and prove worthy of her mission. To accomplish this, she must become an even finer Georgetown.... Unless you can do the best possible job, unless you can do a high type of thing, it is not worthwhile trying. It is not worth a man's life to produce something mediocre."
EDWARD B. BUNN, S.J.

"THEY THAT WAIT upon the Lord shall renew their strength; they shall mount up with wings as eagles; they shall run, and not be weary, and they shall walk, and not faint."
ISAIAH, XL, 31

"BEING A GATHERING of the waters ... a flowage and commingling of peoples in this great basin, from the first red man, Susquehannock, Piscataway, Nanticoke, from the wellsprings of Potomac habitation – to the first white eyes to view, the first white feet to walk upon this green valley – Jesuit, John Smith, Lord Calvert – the trickle growing to a flood tide of whites and the blacks they brought with them – exploring, settling, inhabiting, tilling, fighting, building, polluting, revolting, rebelling, governing, designing... flowing from the wellsprings of history, cleaving through the tangible past, into the present..."
PAUL METCALF, *Waters of Potowmack*

"THIS IS THE SWEETEST and greatest river I have scene, so that the Thames is but a little finger to it." So wrote the Reverend Andrew White, S.J., in 1634 on first viewing the Potomac. This aerial view is taken upriver from Georgetown, where mist and morning sun combine to set the campus in what John Carroll called "one of the most lovely situations that imagine can frame."

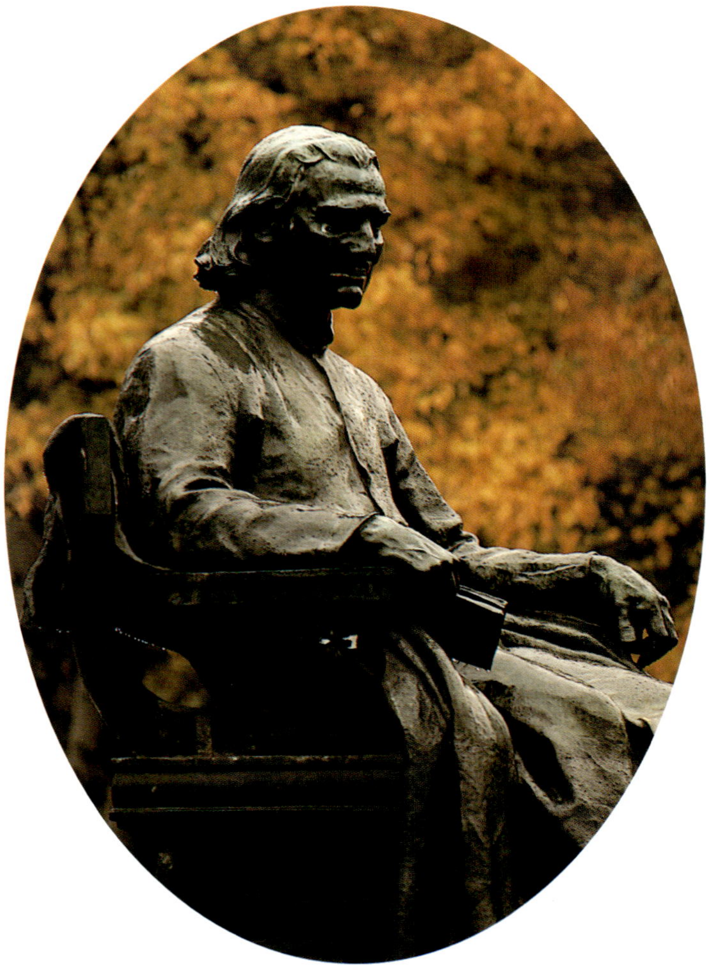